LEGENDS

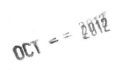

Told by The Old People of Many Tribes

LEGENDS
Told by
The Old People
of Many Tribes

Compiled by Adolf Hungrywolf

Native Voices
Summertown, Tennessee

Native Voices

Book Publishing Company
P.O. Box 99
Summertown, TN 38483
1-888-260-8458

Cover painting & illustration by Ron Mitchell
Cover design by Warren Jefferson
Book design by Jerry Lee Hutchens

12 11 10 09 08   6 5 4 3 2

ISBN 1-57067-116-8
ISBN13 978-1-57067-116-6

Printed in the United States

Hungrywolf, Adolf.
        Legends told by the old people of many tribes / compiled by Adolf Hungrywolf
                p. cm.
        ISBN 1-57067-116-8
1. Indians of North America--Folklore. 2. Indian mythology--North America. 3. Tales--North America. I. Title.
        E98.F6 H85 2001
        398.2'089'97--dc21
                                                2001003619

Book Publishing Co. is a member of Green Press Initiative. We chose to print this title on paper with postconsumer recycled content and processed chlorine free, which saved the following natural resources:

2 trees   78 lbs of solid waste
604 gallons of waste water   145 lbs of greenhouse gases
1 million BTUs

For more information visit: www.greenpressinitiative.org. Savings calculations thanks to the Environmental Defense Paper Calculator at www.papercalculator.org

Contents

Foreword

In the Old Days the often-long Season of Winter was a time spent mostly indoors, around a central fireplace, whether the home was a tipi, an Earth lodge, a Brush lodge, or an igloo. The men were often gone hunting, raiding, or taking care of the Horses. The women were kept busy cooking, sewing, and hauling wood and water. So, it was often left for the Old People in the home—grandfather, or an old aunt—to watch the children and entertain them. They played games, learned songs, and practiced skills that the parents were busy doing. But, as with children everywhere, the favorite pastime was listening to the Old Ones' stories—real or imaginary.

The following stories are a random selection of the countless numbers that have been recorded from some of those Old People. Miles of paper could be filled with more—the ones that follow are just some Good Medicine favorites. So, put another chunk of wood in your stoves, turn up your lamps so you can see good, and gather Your Family around You. Read these stories aloud. You may become inspired to make up some stories of Your own. And have a pleasant evening!

THE STONE BOY

The Creation of Man and Woman
A Sioux Story

The Four Brothers lived together without any woman, so they did the woman's work. One time, as the eldest was gathering wood after nightfall, something ran into his big toe. This pained him but little and he soon forgot it, but his toe began to swell and was soon as big as his head. Then he cut it open and found something in it. He did not know what it was, but his brothers washed it and found that it was a baby girl.

The Four Brothers kept the baby and gave it good food and fine clothes so that it grew to be a beautiful young woman. She could do a woman's work well and quickly and never allowed anyone to leave their tipi cold or hungry. She could dress skins so that they were white and soft and from them make good clothing, upon which she put beautiful ornaments, and each ornament meant something.

Many young men tried to induce her to live with them, but she would not leave the Four Brothers. They told her that they would always keep her as their sister, and they did everything to please her.

The eldest Brother said, "I will go and hunt Deer so that our sister may have the skins to make clothing for herself." He went away and did not return. Then the next eldest Brother said, "I will go and hunt Buffalo so that our sister may have the skins to make robes for herself." He went away and did not return. Then the next youngest Brother said, "I will go and hunt Elk so that our sister may have meat for herself." He too went away and did not return. Then the youngest Brother said, "Sister, our Brothers have gone away and have not returned. I will go and find them." So he went away and did not return.

When the youngest Brother had been gone one Moon, the young woman went to the top of a high hill to mourn, and to seek a vision. While she was mourning she saw a pebble which she looked at for a long time for it was very smooth and white. Then she put the white pebble into her mouth to keep from being thirsty. She fell asleep with the pebble in her mouth and swallowed it. While she slept the vision came to her in the form of a great beast, which told her that the Four Brothers were kept by a stone and that a stone would find them and bring them back to her.

She told this vision to a Shaman and asked him to tell her what it meant. The shaman told her to marry and name her son The Stone. But she would not live with any man, for she remembered how good and kind the Four Brothers were, and she wished to live with them only.

Soon she grew big with child and gave birth to a baby boy. The flesh of this baby was as hard as stone, and she knew that it was mysterious (Wakan) and came from the pebble she had swallowed. She went far away and lived alone with her son. She taught him all the games and songs and all about Roots and Plants and Animals and Birds, so that he was cunning and wise. She gave him fine clothes and good food so that he grew up strong and brave though his flesh was as hard as stone. She would not allow him to hunt or join a war party, for she was afraid he would go away and never return like the Four Brothers.

Each Moon she went to the top of the hill to mourn. When her son had grown to be a man he asked her why she went to

mourn each Moon, and she said to him, "My son, you are now a man, and I will tell you why I mourn." So she told him the story of the Four Brothers, of her coming to them, of how they went away and did not return, of his own birth and the vision of a great beast.

Then she sang this song to him:
> I am a mysterious woman.
> I am like no other woman.
> You are a mysterious man.
> Your flesh is like stone.
> You are the Stone Boy.
> You are the stone the great beast told of.

Then he sang to her:
> I am the Stone Boy.
> I am the stone that will aid you.
> I will bring back your brothers.
> My mother, I will make you happy.

He then said to her, "Mother, I will go to find your brothers. I will bring them to you."

She said, "I am afraid you too will go away and never come back."

He said to her, "What did the great beast tell you? I am the stone."

She said, "Go my son, but first you must be prepared with magic."

She made a great feast and invited a wise Shaman, a wise old woman, a great brave, a great hunter and four maidens as the chief guests, and all the People as common guests. She placed the People as they belonged according to the bands, with her son among the chief guests. When all were satisfied with eating, she stood before the People and told the story of the four brothers: of her coming to them, of their going, of her vision, and the birth and life of her son. She then told them to examine her son that they might know that he was mysterious (Wakan). The People all examined the young man, and when they found that his flesh was hard like stone, they said he was indeed mysterious and that he was the Stone Boy. She then told them that her son was to go in quest of the Four Brothers and she had invited the chief guests so that they would help her to prepare her son with magic for his quest.

The chief guests agreed to do what she should ask of them. The Shaman gave the Stone Boy a charm (Pajuta-wakan-rea) that would keep all harm from him. The old woman gave him a robe on which she had painted a dream which made the robe magical and made anyone who wore it invisible. The warrior gave him a magical spear that would pierce anything, a magical shield that would ward off anything, and a magical club that would break anything. The hunter showed him how to find anything he wanted. His mother made clothes of good Deerskin and the young women put ornaments on them. While ornamenting his clothing, they sang love songs and the Shaman conjured the ornaments (Ca Kina wakan kaga) so that they were magical. On the sides of his moccasins they put mountains so that he could step from hill to hill without touching the valleys; on the tops they put dragonflies so that he could escape all danger; on his leggings they put wolf tracks so that he would never grow weary, on his shirt they put the tipi circle so that he would find shelter anywhere.

He stood before the People, clothed in his magical garments, his shield on his back and his spear and club in his hands. His face was towards the rising Sun. Before him was his mother, on one side the Shaman, warrior, and hunter, and on

the other, the old woman and the four young maidens. He said to his mother, "I will bring the Four Brothers to you." To the young women, "When I return I will take you four as my women." To the men, "What you have taught me I will use to release the Four Brothers." Then turning his face towards the setting Sun he said to the old woman, "I go."

Then the old woman threw the robe about him and he was seen no more, but there was a Wind as if the Thunderbird flew towards the setting Sun. His mother fell on her face as one dead, but the People heard a voice high in the air, clear and loud like the voices of the cranes when they fly towards the region of the Pines, and this is what it said: "A stone shall free the Four Brothers."

When the Stone Boy went from the People, he stepped from hill to hill more swiftly than the Stars (meteors) fall at night. From each hill he looked carefully into the valley so that he saw all there was in every valley, but he saw nothing of the Four Brothers until he came to the high hills far towards the setting Sun.

In the valleys there was much game of every kind and in one valley he found a stone knife that he knew belonged to the eldest Brother. In another valley he found a stone arrowhead that he knew belonged to the next eldest Brother. In a third, he found a stone axe that he knew belonged to the next to the youngest Brother, and in a fourth he found a stone bone breaker that he knew belonged to the youngest Brother. Then he knew he was on the right road to find the Brothers and looked carefully into each valley.

Near the mountains he saw a valley that was barren, with nothing in it but a stone, a tree, and a little brown hill from which he saw smoke rising. He took off his robe and sat down to watch this. Soon a huge Coyote, larger than a Buffalo, came out of the hill and began to jump up very high and yelp very loud. Then the stone began to roll and bump about and the tree began to move from place to place. The stone went to a pool of water and took a drink.

The Stone Boy continued to watch, and soon a growl like Thunder came from the hills beyond. The Coyote, when he heard this growl, jumped very high and fast and yelped and yelled; the stone again moved about and bumped on the ground, the tree moved from place to place, and a little woman came out of the hill and looked towards the growling. Soon a huge Bear as large as a Cloud came over the hills. He walked upright like a man and held some People in his forepaws, and his growl sounded like Thunder. He came into the valley and held the People up to the tree. The Stone Boy saw that each branch of the tree was a Snake. These snakes bit the People as the Bear held them up so that they were paralyzed. When they were still as if they were dead, the bear threw them down on the hard smooth ground and the stone rolled over them and flattened them so that they were like dried Buffalo skins.

Then the little old woman laid them on the little brown hill and the Stone Boy saw that the hill was made of flattened People piled one on top of another. When the People had all been placed on the hill, the Coyote sniffed towards the hill where the Stone Boy stood and jumped and yelled. Then he sniffed and jumped up again; he sniffed very hard, jumped very high, and yelped very loud and the little old woman pointed to that hill and the Bear growled and came to it. But the Stone Boy put on his robe and stepped to another hill. The Bear looked foolish and said, "That must have been a Thunderbird (Wakinyan), a Winged God."

Then the Bear came towards the hill he was on, running very fast, and growling like Thunder. Then the Stone Boy quickly put on his robe and, when the Bear was almost near him, he stepped to another hill. The Bear stopped and looked very foolish and said, "That must have been a Thunderbird that passed by me." Then the Coyote sniffed towards him again and jumped up and down, and the Bear ran towards the hill he was on, but when he got there the Stone Boy stepped to another hill and the Bear looked very foolish and said, I think that is a Thunderbird going by."

Then the Coyote sniffed towards the hill where the Stone Boy stood and again jumped up and down and the tree walked that way and the Stone came also. The Bear growled like very heavy Thunder and came creeping towards the hill, watching everything closely, but when he got near, the Stone Boy stepped to another hill. Then the Bear was afraid, and ran back to the little hill, whining and whimpering, for he thought it was a Thunderbird. Then the little old woman came out of the hill, and the Coyote yelped and jumped up and down and ran around and around, and the branches of the tree squirmed and licked their tongues and hissed like a great Wind. The stone jumped up and down, and every time it came down, it shook the Earth.

Then the Stone Boy stood up and took off his robe and jeered at them and mocked them. They saw him. The old woman screamed and the Coyote yelped louder than ever and jumped up and down, and the tree walked towards him, every snake hissing louder. The stone rolled and tumbled towards him and the Bear came very fast towards him growling like a

Thunder Cloud. When the Bear was very close, he raised his paw to strike, but the Stone Boy shot one of the arrows through his heart and he fell dead.

Then the Coyote came jumping up and down. Every time he jumped up, he went higher and higher, and when he was near enough he jumped up so as to come down on the Stone Boy, but the Stone Boy set his spear on the ground, and when the coyote came down the spear ran through his heart and killed him. Then the stone came rolling and tumbling and smashing everything in its path. When it was about to roll over the Stone Boy and smash him, he raised his war club and struck it a mighty blow and broke it to pieces.

The tree could not walk up the hill, so the Stone Boy went down into the valley, and when he came near the tree the branches began to strike him. But he held up the shield the warrior had given him, and when one the of the snake branches would strike it, its teeth would break off and its head would be smashed. So the Stone Boy danced about the tree and sang and shouted until every branch had smashed itself to death against his shield.

The little old woman then went into the little hill, and the Stone Boy came near it and cried, "Ho, old woman, come out." But the old woman said, "My friend. I am a weak old woman. Have pity on me and come into my tipi."

The Stone Boy saw that the hill was a strange kind of tipi. He found the door, went in, and the old woman said, "My friend, I am a weak old woman, but you are welcome to my tipi. I will get you something to eat and drink." The Stone Boy noticed that her tongue was forked, so he was very wary and watched her closely.

She said, "My Friend, you must be tired. Lie down and rest while I get food for you." The Stone Boy lay down and the old woman passed close, saying to him, "The meat is behind you." As she leaned over him she stabbed him over the heart, but her stone knife broke off when it struck him.

She said, "My Friend, I stumbled and fell on you." The Stone Boy said, "I will sit up, so you will not stumble over me." So she said, "My Friend, sit near the center of the tipi, so I can go about you without stumbling over you."

So the Stone Boy sat near the center of the lodge, and the old woman moved about him. As she passed him she struck him on the head with a warclub, but it only bounced off without hurting him, so she said, "My Friend, you must be hungry. I will make soup for you." She made soup with bad medicine in it and gave it to the Stone Boy, who drank it.

The old woman said, "Ho, you are the one I hate. I am Iya, the evil spirit. I hate all People. I destroy all People. I have given you that which will destroy you. You have swallowed poison. It will kill you. I am Iya the evil one. I know whom you seek. You were hunting for your mother's brothers. They are there in that tipi. They are like tanned skins. You will soon die and I will make a tanned skin of you. I must have a living stone to flatten you out and I must find it. The living stone was my master. He is the only one I feared. He is the only one who could hurt me. No one else can do me any harm. His only relative is a living stone. He is now my master and none other. But you will die from the poison I have given you and I will sing your death song."

She sang:
> A young man would be wise.
> A young man would be brave.
>
> He left the places he knew.
> He came to strange places.

He came to death valley.
He came to Iya's tipi.

He slew Iya's son, the Coyote,
He slew Iya's daughter, the Snake Tree.

He broke the living stone.
He broke Iya's master.

Iya will be revenged on him.
Iya will see him die.

He slew my friend the Bear.
Iya will laugh and see him die.

Then the Stone Boy said, "May I also sing a song?" Iya said "Ho, sing what you will. It is your death song and it is music that will make my heart glad."

The living stone was Iya's master.
The living stone had but one relation.

He had a son that was little.
A pebble that was white as snow.

Iya feared this pebble and stole it.
Feared it because it was white.

Iya carried it into a far away country.
Iya threw it from him on a hilltop.

Where it would not be nourished.
Where it would not be life warmed.

He thought no one would find it.
He thought it would be there forever.

A woman born mysterious.
Found this pebble mysterious.

She gave to it the warmth of life,
The son of the living stone.

The wisest Shaman taught him wisdom.
The bravest warrior taught him bravery.

The oldest woman taught him cunning.
The best of women taught him kindness.

The People taught him justice.
To strive for the right against evil.

He was charmed from harm by the shaman.
He was armed against evil by the warrior.

On his robe was the dream of the old woman.
On his feet was the magic of the young woman.

Thus he came to death's valley.
Thus he came to Iya's tipi.

He slew Iya's friend, the Bear,
Because he enticed the People away.

He slew Iya's son, the Coyote,
Because he did evil only.

He slew Iya's daughter, the Snake Tree,
because her faults were many.

Iya's knife would not harm him.
Iya's club would not kill him.

Iya's broth would not kill him.
It only makes him warm and strong.

I am the pebble you threw away.
I am the Stone Boy, your master.

Then Iya said, "How shall I know you to be my master?"

Stone Boy said, "Do my bidding or I will punish you."

Then Iya said, "I am a weak old woman. Have pity on me and do not punish me."

The Stone Boy said, "Your tongue is forked, and you do not tell the truth. You are not a woman. You are an evil old man. You have pity on no one, but do evil to everyone. Tell me, where are my mother's brothers?"

Iya said, "I do not know. I was only boasting when I said I knew where they were. Have pity on me. Do not make it hard me."

Then the Stone Boy said, "I will have no pity on you. Tell where my mother's brothers are."

Iya said, "I do not know."

Then the Stone Boy seized him by the foot and placed it on the ground and trod on it, and Iya's foot was flattened like a piece of dried skin and he howled with pain. But the Stone Boy demanded he tell where his mother's brothers were, and Iya declared, "I do not know." Then the Stone Boy flattened his other foot in the same way, and Iya sobbed and cried with pain and said he would tell all to the Stone Boy if he would not punish him any further. Iya recognized that the Stone Boy was truly his master.

Iya said, "In ancient times, I found game plentiful in the valleys below here, and good hunters and brave men came here to hunt it. The good men could not be made to do evil at their homes, so I could not do them mischief. So I made a bargain with your father, the living stone, and with the great Bear and brought my sons and daughter with me and we all lived here in this valley. (Iya was a giant; he fought with the living stone. The stone conquered him and became his master. He kept Iya with nothing to eat until he grew smaller and became a little old person.)

"The bargain was that the Bear would go out among the game and when a good man came to hunt, the Bear would show himself and, being so big, the hunters would chase him until they came where they could see my son, who would jump up and down and scare them so that they would fall down with no strength. Then the Bear would take them in his arms and bring them to my daughter who would sting them so that they would be paralyzed. Then the living stone would roll on them and flatten them out like skins and I would heap them on my tipi poles. As they were alive, this would always be a torment for them. In this way I could do mischief to good men.

"We often heard of the four men who lived alone and did women's work and who never did evil to anyone, so that I could not torment them. But they would not hunt or go on the warpath, and we thought they would never come within our power. So I determined to get a woman into their tipi that they might do some evil, but I could not get an ordinary woman among them. Then I tried to break off a branch from my daughter, the Snake Tree, and put it into their tipi, but the branches would not break and the only way I could get a part of my daughter was by digging out a part of the heart of the tree. This I did and placed it near the tipi of the four brothers so that when one of them went to get wood he would step on it and stick it into his toe. These men were so good that when they cared for this child it grew up to be a good woman—as they were good men—but I waited patiently, for when she grew to be a woman I knew they would not live as they had before. When she was a woman they came to hunt game for her, and the Bear enticed

them and they were caught and flattened and are now tormented on my tipi poles.

"When I threw the white pebble away, I knew that no ordinary woman could nourish it into life and growth, and when
your mother grew up to be a woman, I did not think of her
being a mysterious woman who could give life and growth to
the pebble. So my own evil has brought the punishment on me,
for I know that you are my master and that you will not let me
do evil anymore. But those who now lie on my tipi poles will
still be tormented."

Then the Stone Boy said, "Tell me: how can these people
that are on your tipi poles be restored to their natural condition?" Iya said, "I will not." The Stone Boy said, "I am your
master. Tell me or I will punish you." Then Iya said,
"Remember, I am your grandfather, and do not punish me." The
Stone Boy said, "I broke my own father in pieces because he
was evil. Do You think I would spare you because you are my
grandfather?"

Iya said, "I will not tell you."

Then the Stone Boy said, "Give me your hand." He took
Iya's hand and trod on it and it was flattened like a dried skin
and Iya howled with pain. Then the Stone Boy said, "Tell me or
I will flatten your other hand," and Iya said, "I will tell you."

"You must skin the Bear and the Coyote and stretch their
skins over poles so as to make a tight tipi. Then you must gather all the pieces of the broken living stone. You must make a
fire of the wood from the Snake Tree and heat the stones over
this fire, and place them in the tipi. Then get one of the flattened People off the poles of my tipi and place it in the tipi you
have built. Then place the hot stones in the tipi and pour water
over the stones. When the steam rises onto the flattened
Person, he will be as he was before the Bear enticed him."

Then the Stone Boy did as he was told, but the skins of the Bear and the Coyote would not make a full sized tipi, so he made it low and round on top. When he made fire of the Snake Tree, the branches were so fat that one would heat all the stones red hot. He had plenty of fuel to heat the stones as often as he wished. So he placed the flattened People in the sweathouse and steamed them and they became men as they were before they were enticed by the Bear.

He did not know who his mother's brothers were, so he took the arrow he had found and called to all and asked them whose arrow it was. One man said it was his. He told him to stand to one side. He took the stone knife he had found and asked whose it was. A man said it was his and he told him to stand to one side. He then took the plum seed dice he had found and asked whose they were. One man said it was his, and he told him to stand to one side. Then he told the men he had asked to stand aside to look at each other. They did so, and when they had looked at each other they embraced each other, and the Stone Boy knew they were brothers.

Then the Stone Boy told them the story of the four men, of the birth of his mother and how the four men went away and never came back. Then the men said, "We are those four men." The Stone Boy knew that they were his mother's brothers, so he told them the story of his own birth, and they said, "We believe you, because we know the birth of your mother." Then he told them of his preparation to come for them, of his coming and his fight with the Bear, the Coyote, the Stone, and the Snake Tree, and how he was the master of Iya. They said, "We believe you, because the Bear did entice us and the Coyote did jump up and down and the Snake bit us and the Stone did roll over and make us flat like skins and the old woman did spread us on her tipi and we were tormented."

Then the Stone Boy counselled with them as to what he should do to Iya. They advised him to make him flat like a skin, but the Stone Boy said, "There is no Snake Tree to bite him." He came back to Iya and said, "You have been very evil, but now I am your master and I shall punish you for all the evil you have done so that you will always be in torment as you have kept all these People." Iya was a great coward and he begged the Stone Boy to spare him and not punish him. But the Stone Boy said, "I shall flatten you like skin and spread you on a pole."

Then Iya said, "I am Iya, the giant, and I will grow so big that you can not flatten me." He began to grow and grew larger and larger so that he was a great giant. But the Stone Boy began to trample on him. Beginning at his feet, which he had already flattened, he trampled on his legs, so that Iya fell to his knees; he trampled on his thighs so that Iya fell to his buttocks; he trampled on his hips so that great floods of water ran from him. This water was bitter and salty and it soaked into the Earth, and where it comes out in springs or lakes it makes the water very bad and bitter.

Then he trampled his belly, and Iya vomited great quantities of Cherry stones, and the Stone Boy said to him, "What are these Cherry stones?" and Iya said, "They are the People that I have sucked in with my breath when I went about the Earth as a giant." The Stone Boy said, "How can I make these People as they were when you sucked them in with your breath?" Iya said, "Make a fire without smoke." So the Stone Boy got very dry Cotton Wood and made a fire and when it was burned to coals Iya said, "Get some of the hair from the great Bear's skin." He got hair from the great Bear, and Iya said, "Put the hair on the fire," and he put it on the fire. Then there arose a great white smoke, and it was like the smoke from wild Sage branches and leaves. Then Iya said, "Blow this smoke on the Cherry stones." The Stone Boy did so, and Iya said, "This drives away all my power to do these People any harm." Iya said, "Get the hair of many women." The Stone Boy did so and there was a thick blue smoke like the smoke of Sweetgrass and Iya said, "This gives you power to do what you wish to these People."

The Stone Boy said to the People, "Be as you were before Iya sucked you in with his breath." Every Cherry stone arose. They were transformed into more women and children, so that there were a great many People there. These People were all very hungry, so the Stone Boy said to Iya, "What shall I give these people to eat?" Iya replied, "Give them the flesh of the great Bear." So he cut off a piece of the flesh of the great Bear and gave it to a woman. It grew to be a large piece, and this woman cut it in two and gave half of it to another woman. Immediately each of these pieces grew large. Each time a piece was given away it grew large. Then the women built fires and cooked the meat and all feasted and were happy and sang songs.

The People spoke many different languages and could not understand one another, but the Stone Boy could speak to each one in his own language. He addressed some in their own tongue, "Where was your place?" They replied, "Over the Mountains." He said to them, "Go to your People." As he said this to everyone, he gave to the oldest woman of each people a piece of the flesh from the great Bear, so that they had plenty to eat while they traveled. Then the Stone Boy said to his mother's brothers, "Now we will go back to your sister, to my mother, but before we go I will destroy Iya so that he may do no more mischief or hurt the People."

He trod on Iya's chest and his breath rushed out of his mouth and nostrils like a mighty Wind and it whirled and twisted, breaking down trees, tearing up grass, throwing the Water from the Lake, and even piling the Rocks and Earth over the carcasses of the Coyote and the Snake Tree, so that the Thunderbird came rushing through the Air to find out what all this tumult was about. With his Cloud shield he rushed into this great Whirlwind, and while the Lightening spit and flashed from his eyes, he fought the Whirlwind and carried it away into the Sky.

Then the Stone Boy said to Iya, "I will now tread your head and your arms out flat like a dried skin and you shall remain forever here in this evil valley where there is no Tree, nor Grass, nor Water, and where no living thing will ever come near you. The Sun shall burn you and the Cold shall freeze you and you shall feel and think and be hungry and thirsty, but no one shall come near you."

Iya grew so large that he almost lay across the valley. His hands were upon the hill where the Stone Boy first showed himself. When the Stone Boy told him his fate, his hands grasped for something, and he felt the Stone Boy's robe. This he quickly threw over himself and immediately he became invisible. But the Stone Boy saw what he was doing and jumped quickly to trample the breath out of Iya, his mouth gaped wide open. He got the robe over his head before Stone Boy could get his feet on him. When the Stone Boy did trample Iya, he stepped into his mouth, so Iya closed his jaws like a trap and caught both of the Stone Boy's feet between his teeth.

Iya could not hurt the Stone Boy, but he held the feet very tightly between his teeth, and when the Stone Boy drew out one foot, he closed still closer on the other so that when that one was dragged out, the Moccasin was left in Iya's mouth and was invisible and could not be found.

FIRST CREATOR and ONLY MAN
A Mandan Origin Story

It is our custom to tell an old-time story when the corn is ripe. We have a man called Only Man. As he was walking along he came to himself. He stood and thought. A pipe was laying in front of him, over his head flew a Raven. And he sang a song which said, "Where did I come from?" He thought, "Where did I come from? How did I happen to come here?" The Earth about him was Sandy and he could plainly see his own tracks, so he followed them back to see where he came from. He came to a wet spot, then farther on to a great Water, beside which was a plant with spotted leaves. A Buffalo Bug was jumping about in the Sand. The plant said, "I am your mother, it was I that bore you: that is your father," and the Weedmother told Only Man that he was born to arrange matters on the Earth. "Go back to the wet spot and there you will find a tall Weed. That is your pipe. I am just a Weed, this is all I am for. If any-one has a sore eye or stomach trouble, let him take me and boil me up for medicine. Go ahead and create things in the World."

When he came to himself he had a Wolf blanket and a cane with feathers tied to the end. He came to the wet spot, and there grew a tall Tobacco Weed and around it buzzed a Tobacco Fly—buzz, buzz. The Bug said, "I am blowing your Tobacco Plant—use it to smoke." Again he sang the same song—"Where did I come from?" and he pulled up the Tobacco Plant.

As he was trotting along at a gentle pace, another man came up suddenly. The two argued as to which was the older. They agreed: "You lie here and I there and the first one that gets up will be the younger." Only Man said he would leave his cane standing as the other turned about and lay down, and Only Man sang the same song—"Where did I come from?" He went on his way, and traveled over the whole World from one end to the other. Then he thought of his cane, and returning to the spot where it stood, he found it tottering and ready to fall. Grass grew where the other lay. He said, 'This fellow can never get up again!" He took his cane and it became like new and he sang his song and was about to trot away again when the other man got up from the heap of dust where his body had been and said, "I told you that I was older than you!"

The two traveled to create the World. They looked for Mud, but there was Sand alone. They came to a great Lake where there were two Mudhens, a male and a female. They called them over and made them their servants, and the Mudhens dived and brought Mud, and the Men made all creatures. They would throw the Mud in the Air and at once it became a Bird. One Bird had no place to go, so it flew over to the stony places and became a nighthawk. Another stuck its head into the red paint, saying it was hungry, and when it pulled its head out, the head was red, so they said it should have a hard time to get a living out of rotten trees. This was the Woodpecker.

They made many kinds of different Birds and Animals and at last a grandmother Frog came and said, "You are making too many Animals; we must make death so that the first ones may pass away and new ones come." The two said, "You have nothing to say about our business!" and they picked up a stone and hit Grandmother Frog on the back. That is why her legs spread out so. That is how death started, and the child of Grandmother Frog was the first to die. Grandmother Frog came to the Men and said, "I am sorry! Let us take it back and have no deaths!" But the men said, "No, it is impossible; it must be so."

The two said, "Let us improve the Earth—it is all Sand!" So they took the Mud that was left and Only Man took his lump

and smoothed it over the Earth and the Earth was flat. First Creator took a little bit and put it here and there and formed hills and bluffs. Only Man used his cane and leveled the North side of the Earth and made Lakes. First Creator's idea was that when the Snow flies there should be rough Land and Trees and Springs to protect Men and Animals from the cold. First Creator made nothing but Buffalo to roam over the land and in every herd he made a White Buffalo and said that this White One should be precious. From the East this way Only Man created and First Creator created the South side of the Earth. Thus it has been told from generation to generation.

After the creation Only Man was never seen again. First Creator turned him into a Coyote and from him came the Coyote today. He never knew where he came from.

THE WANDERINGS OF THE HOPI PEOPLE
Told by Yukioma
while still of Old Oraibi

(This story tells of the earliest times of Hopi Life here, on this Earth. It is a fitting story for us to hear first, as told by old Yukioma. He was one of the greatest Holy Men remembered by the Hopi. He insisted that Hopi Life should not be distracted by the Ways of other people. His belief led to a major struggle in the old village of Oraibi, which resulted in Yukioma's permanent exile from his ancient home, just one year after he told this story. He led his followers to found a new village — Hotevilla — which soon became the spiritual center of traditional Hopi Life. Because of his strong faith he was, of course, disliked by government officials and by progressive-minded Hopi People. Several times he was imprisoned. One agent had the old man jailed for years, even after describing him in his records as the "American Dalai Lama." Let us hear him speak of the Early Times.)

A very long time ago they were living down below in the underworld. Everything was good there at that time. That way of living was good down there. Everything was good, everything grew well; it rained all the time, everything was blossoming. That is the way it was, but by and by it became different. The chiefs commenced to do bad. Then it stopped raining and they only had very small crops and the winds began to blow, People became sick. By and by it was like it is here now, and at last the People participated in this. They, too, began to talk bad and to be bad. And then those who have not a single heart (the Hopi use the name Two-Hearts for those Persons who are possessed by evil spirits), the sorcerers, that are very bad, began to increase and became more and more. The People began to live the way we are living now, in constant contentions. Thus they were living. Nobody would listen anymore. They became very bad. They would take away the wives of the chiefs.

The chiefs hereupon became angry and they planned to do something to the People, to take revenge on them. They began to think of escaping. So a few of the chiefs met once and thought and talked about the matter. They had heard some sounds away up, as of footsteps, as if somebody was walking there, and about that they were talking. Then the Kik-mongwi, who had heard the sounds above, said that they wanted to investigate above and see how it was there, and then if the one above wanted them, they wanted to try to go out. So the others were willing too. They wanted to find out about that, and then, if they were permitted, they wanted to move up there. So they were now thinking who should find out. So they made a Pawaokaya (a certain kind of Bird), sang over it, and thus brought it to life. "Why do you want me?" the Bird said. "Yes," the chief said, "we are not living well here, our hearts are not light, and they are troubling us here, and now I have been thinking about these few children of mine here and we want to see whether we can find some other way of living. Away above there somebody seems to be walking, and now we thought maybe you could go up there and see about that and find out for us. That is the reason we want you." "All right," the Pawaokaya said, "all right, I shall go up there and find out about it." Hereupon the chief planted a looqo (a kind of tall tree), but they saw that it did not reach up, but that its point was turning downward. Hereupon they planted a reed by the side of the pine and that reached up. They then told the Pawaokaya to go up now and if he should find anybody to tell him and then if he were willing they would go.

So the Pawaokaya ascended, flying in circles upward around these two ladders. When he came up to the top he found an opening there, through which he went out. After he came out he was flying around and around, but did not find anybody, so he returned to the opening again and came down. As he was very tired he fell down upon the ground before the chiefs. When he was somewhat revived they asked him, "Now, what have you found out?" "Yes," he said, "I went through there and there was a large space there, but I did not find anybody. When I did not find anybody I became hungry and thirsty and very tired, so I have come back now." "Ishohi! (Oh!)" they said. "Very well, now who else will go?" and they were thinking. "Somebody else shall go," they said, and they kept thinking about it.

So they made another bird, but this time a small one, and when they were singing over it it became alive. When it had become alive they saw that it was a Humming-Bird, which is very small, but very swift and strong. "Why do you want me," the Bird said. "Yes," they said, "our children here are not with good hearts. We are not living well here; we are living here in trouble. So we want you to go up there for us and see what you can find out, and if the one up there is kind and good, we think of going up there, and that is the reason why we want you. So you go up there; you hunt somebody, and if he is gentle and kind, we shall go up there." So the Bird flew upward, circling around the two trees, went through the opening and flew around and around, and not finding anybody also became tired and came back. He flew lower and lower and alighted in front of the chiefs, exhausted. When he had somewhat revived, they

asked him: "Now then, what have you heard, what have you found out?"

"Yes," he said, "yes, I flew around there that way and became tired and exhausted and have come back." "Ishohi!" they said again, "now then, we shall send somebody else."

(The same thing again took place when the chiefs sent up a Hawk. When the Hawk came back they decided to try again — a fourth and last time.)

So they made another one, and sang over it again. While they were singing over it it became alive, and it was the Motsni. "Why do you want me?" the latter asked. "Yes," they said, "our children here do not listen to us, they have hard hearts, and we are living in trouble here. So we have been thinking of leaving here, but these here have not found anybody there, so you go up too, and you find out for us. And, if you find someone there who is kind and gentle and has a good heart, why you tell us and we shall go up there." So he flew up too, having passed through the opening, he kept flying around and looking about, as he was very strong. Finally he found the place where Oraibi now is, but there were no houses there yet, and there somebody was sitting, leaning his head forward, and as the Motsni came nearer he moved it to the side a little. Finally he said: "Sit down, you that are going around here, sit down. Certainly you are going around here for some reason. Nobody has seen me here yet." "Yes," the Motsni said, "down below we are not living well, and the chiefs there have sent me up here to find out, and now I have found you, and if you are kind, we have thought of coming up here, since I now have found you. Now you say, you tell me if you are willing, and I shall tell them so, and we will come up here." This one whom the Motsni found was Skeleton (masauwuu). "Yes," he said, "now this is the way I am living here. I am living here in poverty. I have not anything; this is the way I am living here. Now, if you are willing to live here that way, too, with me and share this life, why come, you are welcome." "All right," the Motsni said, "whatever they say down there, whatever they say. Now, I shall be off." "All right," Skeleton said, whereupon the Motsni left.

So he returned and descended to where the chiefs were sitting, but this one did not drop down, for he was very strong, and he came flying down to them. "What have you found out?" they asked the Bird. "Yes," he said, "I was up there and I have found him away off. But it is with you now; he also lives there poorly, he has not much, he is destitute. But if you are satisfied with his manner of living, why you are welcome to come up there." "All right," they said, and were happy. "So that is the way he is saying, so he is kind, we are welcome, and we are going."

At that time there were all kinds of People living down there, the White Man, the Paiute, the Pueblo; in fact, all the different kinds of People except the Zuni and the Kohonino, who have come from another place. Of all these People some whose hearts were not very bad had heard about this, and they had now assembled with the chiefs, but the greater part of the People, those whose hearts were very bad, were not present. They now decided that they would leave. So during the four days those who knew about it secretly told some of their friends whose hearts also were at least not very bad, that after four days they were going to leave. So the different chiefs from the different kinds of People assembled with small parties on the morning of the fourth day, after they had had their morning meal. They met at the place where they were appointed to meet, and there were a good many. "We are a great many," the chief said, "maybe there will be some here among them whose heart is not single. Now, no more must come, this is enough." So they commenced to climb up the reed, first the different chiefs, the Village Chief, who was also at the same time the Soyal Chief, the Flute Chief, the Horn Chief, Agave Chief, Singer Chief, Wuwuchim Chief, Rattlesnake Chief, Antelope Chief, Marau Chief, Lagon Chief, and the Warrior Chief. And then the People followed and a great many went out. By this time the People in the lower world had heard about this, and they now came crowding from all sides towards the trees. When the Village Chief above there saw that so many were coming he called down to stop. "Some of those Popwaktu," he said, "are going to come up too, I think, so that is enough, stop now!" He then commenced to pull up the reed so that a great many People that were still on it dropped back.

So they now moved on a little bit to the rim or edge of the opening, and there they gathered, and there were a great many of them. The Village Chief now addressed them and said: "Now this many we have come out, now we shall go there, but we want to live with a single heart. Thus long we have lived with bad hearts. We want to stop that. Whatever that one there (referring to the Motsni) tells us, we want to listen to, and the way he says we shall live." Thus he instructed them.

In a little while the child of the chief, a small boy, became sick and died. "Ishohi!" the chief said, "a Powaka has come out with us," and they were thinking about it. Then he made a ball of fine meal and threw it upward and it alighted on the head of a maiden. So he went there and grabbed her, saying: "So you are the one. On your account my child has died. I shall throw you back again." He then lifted her to the opening. "I am going to throw you down here," he said, "you have come out with us and we shall now live in the same way here again." But she did not want to. "No," she said, "you must not throw me down, I want to stay with you, and if you will contend with one another again I shall always talk for you (be on your side). Now, you go and look down there and you will see your child going around down there." So he looked down and there he saw his child running around with the others. "That is the way it will be," the maiden said to the chief; "if anyone dies, he will go down there and he will remain there only four days, and after the four days he will come back again and live with his People." Hereupon the chief was willing that she should remain and he did not throw her down, but he told her that she could not go with them right away. When they should leave, when they had slept, after the first day she might follow them. So she remained there near the opening.

Hereupon the Warrior Chief looked around all over and he found out that towards one side it was always cold. It was at this time dark yet, so Spider Woman took a piece of white woven cloth and cut a large round piece out of it on which she made a drawing. She was assisted by the Flute priest. They sang some songs over it, and Spider Woman then took the disk away towards the East. Soon they saw something rise there, but it did not become very light yet, and it was the Moon. So they said they must make something else. Spider Woman and the Flute priest then took a piece of buckskin, cut a circular piece out of it, and made on it a drawing of the Sun symbol, as is still used by the Flute priest today. They sang over this, whereupon Spider Woman took that away and in a little while something rose again, and now it became light and very warm. But they had rubbed the yolks of eggs over this Sun symbol and that is what makes it so very light, and that is why the Chickens know when it is light and yellow in the morning, and crow early at the Sunrise, and at noon, and in the evening, and now they know all about the time. And now the chief and all the People were happy because it was light and warm.

The chiefs now made all different kinds of blossoms and plants and everything. They now thought of starting and scattering out. The language then spoken was the Hopi language. This language was dear and sacred to the Hopi chief, and he wanted to keep it alone to himself and for the Hopi, but did not want the People who would scatter out to take this language along, and so he asked the Mockingbird, who talks everything, to give the different People a different language. This the Mockingbird did, giving to one party one language, to another party another language, and so on, telling them that these languages they should henceforth speak. Hereupon they sat down to eat a common meal, and the chief laid out a great many corn ears of different lengths which they had brought from the underworld. "Now," he said, "you choose of these corn ears before you start." So there was a great wrangle over these corn ears, every one wanting the longest ears, and such People as the Navajo, Ute, Apache, etc., struggled for and got the longest corn-ears, leaving the small ones for the Hopi, and these the chief took and said: "Thanks, that you have left this for me. Upon this we are going to live. Now, you that took the long corn ears will live on that, but they are not corn, they will be kwahkwi, lahu, and such grasses that have seed." And that is the reason why these People rub out the tassels of those grasses now and live on them; and the Hopi have corn, because the smaller ears were really the corn.

The chief had an elder brother, and he selected some of the best foods that tasted well, such as nookwiwi (a stew of mutton, shelled corn, etc.), meats, etc. They were now ready to start, and then the chief and his elder brother talked with each other and agreed that the elder brother should go with a party ahead towards the Sunrise, and when he would arrive there he should touch the Sun, at least with his forehead, and then remain and live where the Sun rises. But they should not forget their brethren, they should be looking this way, towards the place where they would settle down. A So-Wuhti (old woman — grand mother) went with each party. Each party also took a stone upon which there were some marks and figures, and that fitted together. They agreed that if the Hopi should get into trouble again, and live again the same way as they did in the lower world, the elder brother should come back to them and discover the Powakas who caused the trouble, and cut off their heads.

The elder brother and his party started first, and they became the White Men as they traveled Eastward. The chief and his party started next, both taking a Southern route. The maiden that had been found to be a Powaka, and who had been left behind at the opening, followed these two parties after they had left.

The People hereupon formed different parties, each party following a certain chief, and all traveling Eastward. They usually stopped for longer or shorter periods at certain places, and then traveled on again. For this reason there are so many ruins all over the country. The Pueblo People also passed through about here where the Hopi now live. The White Men were more skillful than the others and got along better. Spider Woman, who was with them, made Horses and Burros for them, on which they traveled when they got tired, and for that reason they went along much faster. The party that brought Powak-mana (the evil girl) with them settled down at Palatkwapi, where they lived for quite a while, and these did not yet bear a particular clan name.

The other parties traveled different routes and were scattered over the country, each party having a chief of its own. Sometimes they would stay one, two, three, or four years at one place, wherever they found good fields or springs. Here they would raise crops so that they had some food to take with them when they continued their journeys, and then moved on again. Sometimes when they found good fields but no water they would create springs with a Bauypi. This is a small perforated vessel into which they would place certain herbs, different kinds of stones, shells, a small balolookong, Bahos, etc., and bury it. In one year a spring would come out of the ground where this was buried. During this year, before their spring was ready, they would use rainwater, because they understood how to create rain. When they continued their journeys they usually took such a Bauypi out of the ground and took it with them.

Before any of the parties had arrived at the place where the Hopi now live they had begun to become bad. Contentions arose among the parties. They began to war against each other. Whenever a certain party possessed something, another party would attack and kill them on account of those possessions. For that reason some of them built their villages on top of the bluffs and mesas, because they were afraid of other parties. Finally some of them arrived at Muenkapi (Moencopi a little stream about fifty miles North-West of Oraibi). These were the Bear Clan, the Spider Clan, Hide Strap Clan, Blue-Bird Clan, and the Fat Cavity Clan; all of which had derived their names from a dead Bear upon which these different parties had come as they were traveling along.

While these parties lived near Muenkapi for some time another party had gone along the Little Colorado river, passed by the place that is now called the Great Lakes, and arrived at Shongopavi, where they started a village at the place where now the ruins of old Shongopavi are, east of the present village. These People were also called the Bear Clan, but they were a different Bear People from those living at Muenkapi at that time. Shongopavi was the first village started. When these Bear People arrived at Shongopavi, Skeleton was living at the place where Oraibi now is, where he had been living all the time. The clan that had stopped North-East of Muenkapi soon moved to the place where Muenkapi now is, but did not remain there long. The Bear Clan, the Hide Strap Clan, and the Blue-Bird Clan soon moved on towards Oraibi. When the Spider Clan arrived at Muenkapi they made marks or wrote on a certain bluff East of Muenkapi, saying that this place should always belong to the Hopi, that no one should take it away from them, because there was so much water there. Here the Hopi should always plant.

Soon after the Spider clan had moved on towards Oraibi the Snake clan arrived. When these Snake People saw the writing on the bluff they said: "Somebody has been writing here that they wanted to own this. Let us write also that we want to own this here, too." So they wrote the same thing on the bluff. After they had left the place, the Burrowing Owl Clan arrived, and they also wrote the same thing on the bluff. But they all had heard that Skeleton was living where Oraibi now is, and so they all traveled on towards Oraibi. When the Bear Clan arrived at Natuwanpika, a place a very short distance West of Kuiwanva (a mile North-West of Oraibi), Skeleton came to meet them there. "We have arrived here," the Hon-wungwa said, "we would like to live here with you, and we want you to be our chief. Now what do you think about it? Will you give us some land?" But Skeleton replied: "No, I shall not be chief. You shall be chief here, you have retained your old life. You will be the same here as you were down in the underworld. Someone that is Powaka has come out with you and it will be here just the same as it was down there when he comes back here. But when the White Man, your elder brother, will come back here and cut off the heads of the bad ones, then I shall own all this land of mine myself. But until then you shall be chief. I shall give you a piece of land and then you live here."

Hereupon he stepped off a large tract of land, going East of where they were, and then descending the mesa West of Koqochmovi, then towards the present trail towards Oraibi, up the trail, past the present village site, down the mesa on the West side, along the trail towards Momoshvavi, including that spring, and back up the mesa. This piece of land he allotted to the Bear Clan. The leader of the Bear Clan now asked him where he lived. He said he lived over there at the bluff of Oraibi, and that is where they should live also. So this clan built its houses right East of the bluff of Oraibi where there are now the ruins.

The Bear Clan brought with them the Soyal cult, the Aototo, and the Soyal Katsinas. Soon other clans began to arrive. When a clan arrived usually one of the new arrivals would go to the village and ask the village chief for permission to settle in the village. He usually asked whether they understood anything to produce rain and good crops, and if they had any cult, they would refer to it and say, "Yes, this or this we have, and when we assemble for this ceremony, or when we have this dance it will rain. With this we have traveled, and with this we have taken care of our children." The chief would then say, "Very well, you come and live in the village." Thus the different clans arrived. While these different clans arrived in Oraibi, other clans were arriving in Walpi and Mishongnovi, and settling up those villages. When a new clan arrived, the village chief would tell them: "Very well, you participate in our cult and help us with the ceremonies," and then he would give them their fields according to the way they came. And that way their fields were all distributed.

One of the first clans to arrive with those mentioned was the Bow Clan, which came from the South-West. When the village chief asked the leader of this clan what he brought with him to produce rain, he said, "Yes, we have here the Shaalako Katsinas, the Tangik Katsinas, the Tukwunang Katsina, and the Shawiki Katsina. When they dance it usually rains." "Very well," the village chief said, "you try it." So the Aoat-wungwa arranged a dance. On the day before the dance it rained a little, and on the last day when they had their dance it rained fearfully. All the washes were full of water. So the village chief invited them to move to the village and gave them a large tract of land. He told them that they should have their ceremonies first. This was the Wuwuchim ceremony, the chief of the Bow Clan being the leader of this ceremony. So this ceremony was the first one to take place.

Then followed the Soyal Ceremony, in charge of the village chief. And then in the Baho month the Snake and the Flute ceremonies, which change about every two years. The Snake cult was brought by the Snake Clan, the Antelope cult by the Blue-Bird Clan, and the Flute cult by the Spider Clan. The Lizard, which also arrived from the North-West, brought the Marau cult, and the Parrot Clan the Lagon cult. Others came later. Small bands living throughout the country when they could hear about the People living in Oraibi would sometimes move up towards Oraibi and ask for admission to live in the village. In this way the villages were built up slowly.

At that time everything was good yet. No wicked ones were living in the village at that time. When the Katsinas danced it would rain, and if it did not rain while they danced, it always rained when the dance was over, and when the People would

have their kiva ceremonies it would also rain. But at that time they had not so many Katsinas (about 250, nowadays). There were only the Hopi Katsinas, which the Hopi brought with them from the under-world. They were very simple but very good. People at that time lived happily, but by this time the Popwaktu had increased at Palatkwapi. The one Powaka maiden that had come with these People from the under-world had taught others her evil arts. And so these wicked ones had increased very much until finally Palatkwapi was destroyed by a great water produced by the Balolokongs. Nearly all the People were destroyed, but a few succeeded in reaching dry land in the flood and they were saved.

They traveled North-Eastward and finally came to Matovi, and from there to Walpi. From Walpi they scattered to the different villages, teaching their evil arts to others. They would put sickness into the People so that the People contracted diseases and died. They also turned the Ute People and the Apache, who used to be friends of the Hopi, into their enemies, so that after that these tribes would make wars on the Hopi. They also caused contentions among the Hopi. The Navajo also used to be friends of the Hopi, but these Popwaktu would occasionally call the Ute and the Apache to make raids on the Hopi. They also turned the Navajo into our enemies, and then the White Men came and made demands on the Hopi. The White Men are also called here by these Popwaktu, and now the White Men are worrying the Hopi also.

But the Hopi are still looking towards their elder brother, the one that arrived at the Sunrise first, and he is looking from there this way to the Hopi, watching and listening how they are getting along. Our old men and ancestors have said that some White Men would be coming to them, but they would not be the White Men like our elder brother, and they would be worrying us. They would ask for our children. They would ask us to have our heads washed (baptized), and if we would not do what they asked us they would beat us and trouble us and probably kill us. But we should not listen to them, we should continue to live like the Hopi. We should continue to use the food of the Hopi and wear the clothes of the Hopi. But those Popwaktu of the Hopi would help the White Men, and they would speak for the White Men, because they would also want to do just the same as those White Men would ask them to do. And now it has come to that, our forefathers have been prophesying that. We are now in trouble. Our children are taken away from us, and we are being harassed and worried.

CROW NECKLACE
and His MEDICINE CEREMONY

A Hidatsa Story

There was a party of Gros Ventre Indians who went out for a hunt from Knife River where the old camp was, and while they were hunting, the Assiniboins came and attacked the hunters. Some got away and were saved. A young man among them looked for his sister and could not find her. So he trailed them to their camp. This man was an Assiniboin who had been as a little boy captured by the Gros Ventre and made a slave. The girl called him brother, but was not really related to him. When all was quiet at night he went through the camp to look for his sister. He came to a big tipi and heard talking. Looking through a hole, he saw two men wounded whom he recognized as his own brothers. Now he had shot two Assiniboin in the conflict (and he recognized these two as the ones he shot). Drawing his robe over his head, he entered and sat down beside their father, who was his father too. The wounded men told their father to fill his pipe and smoke with the stranger. The boy had not forgotten his own language, so he spoke to the old man and said, "Father, it is I." When he told what had happened to him, the father put his hands about his neck and fainted; the mother did the same. When he told them it was he who had shot the two brothers, they all laughed over it. He told them that he was looking for his sister, and the wounded men advised the father to call in the chiefs and tell them about her. So the chiefs arranged not to move camp for four days, but to have a feast and call together all the slaves taken from the Gros Ventres and let them eat. Then they had a dance called the scalp-dance, but the sister was not there. According to the old custom, slaves are supposed to belong to the tribe by which they are captured, so the slaves too got up and danced with them. All the slaves knew the young man. They called him "Crow Necklace."

Before the four days were passed he said to the slaves, "Go steal some moccasins and dry meat and one of these nights we will run away." On the last of the four nights they were all prepared. They stole sinew and cut pieces of Buffalo hide from the tents for moccasins. It was storming when they left—young women, old, and children, the young women carrying the children on their backs and they ran North instead of East in the direction from which they came. Coming to a dry Lake, they lay down in the deep Grass and the Snow covered them. Meanwhile, the Assiniboin discovered their absence and tracked after them but could not find them. They came to the Lake but, seeing nothing of them, went home except one who stood looking. Crow Necklace crept up and killed him and took his scalp.

That night they went until daylight, traveling North-East until they came to another dry Lake thick with Grass. There they stayed all Day. Four days they traveled in the night and hid all day. By this time they were up at the head waters. From there they came around toward the Missouri River and came out at a place we call "Timber Coulee." At that time it was full of timber. Crow Necklace was about to push down an old Tree which had an Owl's nest on top. An old Owl said, "Don't push that tree or my young ones will get cold. We are the ones who have helped you get around to your home again. It will be best for you to go back to your own tribe: there you will find a chief's daughter waiting to marry you." So when they wanted him to marry some of the women he refused and said, "No! the young ones are my sisters and the old ones are my mothers."

The owl directed him, "After leaving this place, go directly to the Short Missouri to camp, then on to Wood-trap (right across the river west of here). Here all the Spirits will set traps to catch all kinds of wild Animals for you to eat. When you get there, build a tipi out in the bush. Go inside and do not go out, and they will bring you meat themselves." So they did this—fixed up nice and went in. Outside they could hear the noise of butchering going on around them. When the noise ceased they went out and found meat cut up or wrapped in hides and laid up on scaffolds. The Owl told Crow Necklace that they were now not far from the tribe—at the next move they would reach home. The next day they moved until they came to a high hill. Crow Necklace fixed up a skull and painted their faces black. As they approached, they saw a woman crying on top of a hill and someone pointed her out to Crow Necklace; it was his sister. He called to her, and when she saw him she fainted. Then the whole camp came out to meet them and everybody made much of Crow Necklace. He told the story of their adventures and brought the food for them to eat.

All the hides he had asked to have tanned in order to make Medicine after he got back home. Among them was a White Buffalo hide. So after he had married a chief's daughter, as had been foretold, he made Medicine in order to understand all the mysterious beings and leave out none of them. And that cost him anything he had prepared—a hundred moccasins, a hundred robes, a hundred blankets—everything in hundreds.

THE STORY OF HUNGRY WOLF

An Assiniboin Story

A young man and his wife were up hunting in the breaks North of Little Missouri, back by Kildeer Mountains. The man camped there with his wife. He was successful as a hunter, and his wife cured the hides and fried strips of jerked meat. One night he told her to pack up everything, as the next day they would be leaving. The next morning early he went out to get some fresh meat for the journey and returned with parts of a Rocky Mountain Sheep and its hide, which the People regard as very valuable. He found the packages on the scaffold just as he had left them, but his wife and dog were gone.

Circling about the tent he found no trace, but the fourth day he found a few tracks of men. With the tracks of men were the tracks of his wife and dog heading South. He went back to camp and pounded the meat and roasted the fattest meat and stored it away in bags to eat on the way, then he followed the trail. The fugitives hid their trail by spreading out and then coming together again, so that the tracks were hard to follow. Thus he followed a party which he judged to consist of twelve persons. When he came to Looks-Like-a-Chicken-Tail butte, he turned South-West and saw smoke rising from a camp. He waited until Sunset, then walked into the camp. There he stood a while, considering. He covered his head with his robe, carrying bow and arrows under his robe in case of attack. He could see young men walking about engaged in courting. As he went from tent to tent listening for signs of his wife, their Dog ran out from a tent and jumped about its master. He gave it meat. The Dog returned inside the tent, whined, wagged its tail and ran out again to its master. He went and stood in the doorway.

Within he could see his wife sitting. An old woman came in, and to his surprise his wife spoke to her in Gros Ventres. She was an old woman who had also been taken prisoner and had lived among the enemy until she was old.

He surveyed the situation of the camp. On the outskirts was a ravine where a spring had made a small pond. A trail led down to this pond, made by the women going after water. Beside the pond grew Beaver Grass, long and fine, right down to the water's edge. There he hid, hoping that when his wife came down to get water, they might plan an escape. His plan was to start in the night, go westward toward the mountains, and come back home. In the morning a stream of women came down after water. At noon fewer came. In the early afternoon he saw the Dog coming down the bank wagging his tail. His wife came to the edge of the spring and, standing on a stone, leaned over to dip water. He said, "Stay just where you are, my own heart, I heard you talking last night with the old woman. My plan is for you to come out here when everyone is asleep. The People will expect us to go back to our old camp, so we will go towards the mountains and live on game on the way home. Afterwards we will go back and get our packages at the camp."

He lay behind the grass. In the evening after the women who came down after water had left, the men came down and encircled the pond. They overpowered him, took away his bow and arrows and carried him away to a tent and gave him food. His wife came and looked into the tent. He said, "I believe that it is you who have betrayed me."

They dug two holes in a circle, set in two posts, lanced his muscles next to the bone at wrists and ankles, stretched his arms and legs to the posts; then they scalped him, and tying the scalp to a long pole, they sent out drummers and all came out and danced the victory dance and carried his scalp about on the pole. They brought firewood and made a pile of it before and behind him, intending to burn him; but just then an old man came out who seemed to have authority, and stopped the dancing and made signs towards Sun, but his words were unintelligible. The old Gros Ventre woman came to him and said, "My dear, it is all your wife's fault. You communicated with her when she went down to get water. When she returned she told the camp that there was a Corn Man down in the waterhole. I was taken away when young by these people and have been here ever since. I married and have children and grandchildren and hence have been contented to live among them. When they brought the Gros Ventre woman here, as she was one of our tribe, I went over to her tent to comfort her. It was your wife who advised that you be captured and tortured to death. You cannot expect a woman to keep a secret. The man who spoke to People told them that when we fight and kill an enemy we kill him quickly. He said, 'The great God in the Heavens is looking down upon us. If you burn this man, that Great Spirit will some day avenge this deed. He will punish us. Let us wait and see what will happen.'"

The next day when the People broke camp, some came over and pierced his eyes; then they left him and went away. For four days he remained hanging. On the fourth day toward dusk he heard an Owl hooting. He came nearer and hooted again. He could hear the grass rustling as from a man walking close to him. The steps stopped in front of him and a man said, "My son, the hooting of the Owl was myself. I have come to see what I can do to restore your sight." He heard him spitting on his hands and rubbing the palms together. The man told him to look up, and he rubbed the palms of his hands over his eyes, and his eyesight was restored. The man told him, "Fear not, the torture from which you are suffering has been caused by your wife. But you shall live and see your home again. You must stand and listen at daybreak when Sun comes over the hill and you will hear the Earth trembling and the sound of something falling to Earth. That which you hear falling and whose vibration you feel is white clay, which is being made for you in the Sky and dropped from the Sky to Earth. You will find it near Red Grass butte beside Knife River. When you get home, when you give a dance, let the Grandma society clean a lodge site and pile the grass in the center as a symbol of your standing here. Strip a cane in four places as a symbol of the four days you have stood here without food and water. It will be a token of long life and prosperity. Give another such cane to a brother or some relative. The two canes are symbols of the two torture posts. There shall be a circle for the Wolf society and the old scouts shall circle around you. Take one Winter to prepare all the articles for the dance. Ask all your friends and relatives to help you. They shall make arrows and give them as payment to the scouts who sing and tell of their exploits and they shall give them to their sons and young relatives to use against those who tortured you. Next year you will find these same People camping here, and you shall kill a hundred of them. You shall capture this old Gros Ventre woman and your wife. Save their lives, but do not make the woman your wife again. You shall marry the daughters of your chief. Teach your warriors to use in the battle shields made of buffalo hide hardened by burning with hot stones."

The Owl Man told him that in the morning he would see Wolf-of-the-Sunset dancing with his warriors. He must watch their dress and learn their songs and make this dance a part of his Mystery. In the morning the Wolf-of-the-Sunset came with his warriors, who were a pack of Wolves. They freed him and took him into their company by the name of Hungry Wolf. The

scouts come in the rear. The Raven as he flies over the country seeing all that is going on is like the scout. It was the Raven who had told the Owl how the man was being tortured and had reported it to Wolf-of-the-Sunset. That is why the two men who led in the Wolf Dance and impersonate Wolf-of-the-Sunset and Hungry Wolf wear Raven feathers. Just as the Wolves do for the fasters in the dance, so the Wolves came that day, removed the rawhides that bound him and gave him the feast of fat of the Buffalo to eat. They said, "This will drive away the pain of the torture. When your People kill a Buffalo, after skinning the breastbone, they must take a mouthful of the fat, and whatever their sickness this will cure it." They took fat and anointed his wounds in his arms and feet and on the forehead. They daubed him with white clay all over and then, as a sign of healing, they made scratches with their fingernails in the clay on his calves, his forearm, and on his forehead, thus leaving the clay in streaks. This white clay is used at the Wolf ceremony. The heap in the center of the clearing is the symbol of his torture. When they dance about, they must go over to the right side (and dance from the right to the left) in order to insure long life and prosperity; if they start from the left, it is a sign of misery. So when People smoke, the pipe is handed to the extreme right of the circle and then handed around.

The Wolves told him to follow them. When he got over the divide, he found a Buffalo butchered and blood and kidney, liver and guts, laid aside for him to eat raw. The Wolf placed on his head a piece of hide from the Buffalo's head, sang a song, and his torn scalp was healed and the hair turned the color of his own hair. Thus he reached home. Then he climbed up to his old lodge, face to the West, and said "Hee-hay!" (which signifies "Listen!"). He spoke to the Wolves of the West and said, "This Winter I shall have bedding (Buffalo hides) scraped for you and shall bring the Wolves into my lodge (meaning warriors) in order to conquer my enemies." Taking hunters and Dogs, he returned to his old camp and brought back his bundles. He placed food in those lodges where the societies met and in return they gave arrows and other things for the ceremony. He sent one of his sisters to the chief's lodge and asked for the hand of the chief's two daughters in marriage.

During the Winter he instructed the Wolves in the scout songs he had learned from the Wolves. In the Summer he sent for the white clay and had the dance performed. After this he called for the young men through the announcer and for the old

men who had endurance and speed and provided them with moccasins and provisions for the war path. On the outskirts of the village the warriors assembled. When they reached the butte, he was told that this was the place to mine the bright red ochre which is to be found there in pockets. Since he had too many scouts, he selected from the forty-five the fourteen who were the fastest runners. They had to run one by one between the two goals while the rest in the center tried to catch them. This is called "running by." If anyone was caught before he reached the opposite goal, he was put out. They went on and sent out scouts ahead. They reported a hundred and fifty tents. There were 2500 persons in the village. They got close to camp, whooped, and attacked at daybreak. After a hundred warriors had been killed, he gave the signal to stop by waving his robe in the air. No women or children were killed, or any old people. The old Gros Ventre woman and the young man's wife were taken. The old woman was allowed to go back to the tribe, the wife was brought back to the village. No one would marry her, and it was she who introduced harlotry.

In the village they danced the greatest victory dance ever known. Hungry Wolf lived to old age and had children and grandchildren. The mystery he conferred upon his son, and so it was handed down from generation to generation.

ORIGIN OF THE SWEAT LODGE

A Nez Perce Story

Long ago, in the days of the Animal People, Sweat Lodge was a man. He foresaw the coming of Human Beings, the real inhabitants of the Earth. So one day he called all the Animal People together to give each one a name and to tell him his duties.

In the council, Sweat Lodge stood up and made a speech: "We have lived on Earth for a long while, but we shall not be in our present condition much longer. A different People are coming to live here. We must part from each other and go to different places. Each of you must decide whether you wish to belong to the Animal beings that walk, fly or creep or those that swim. You may now make your choice."

Then Sweat Lodge turned to Elk. "You will first come this way, Elk. What do you wish to be?"

"I wish to be what I am — an Elk."

"Let us see you run or gallop," said Sweat Lodge.

So Elk galloped off in a graceful manner, and then returned.

"You are all right," decided Sweat Lodge, "You are an Elk."

Elk galloped off, and the rest saw no more of him.

Sweat Lodge called Eagle to him and asked, "What do you wish to be, Eagle?"

"I wish to be just what I am — an Eagle."

"Let us see you fly," replied Sweat Lodge.

Eagle flew, rising higher and higher and with hardly a ripple on his outstretched wings.

Sweat Lodge called him back and said to him, "You are an Eagle. You will be king over all the Birds of the Air. You will soar in the Sky. You will live on the crags and peaks of the highest Mountains. The Human Beings will admire you."

Happy with that decision, Eagle flew away. Everybody watched him until he disappeared in the Sky.

"I wish to be like Eagle," Bluejay told Sweat Lodge.

Wanting to give everyone a chance, Sweat Lodge said again, "Let us see you fly."

Bluejay flew into the air, trying to imitate the easy, graceful flight of eagle. But he failed to keep himself balanced and was soon flapping his wings.

Noticing his awkwardness, Sweat Lodge called Bluejay back to him and said, "A Jay is a Jay. You will have to be contented as you are."

When Bear came forward, Sweat Lodge said to him, "You will be known among Human Beings as a very fierce Animal. You will kill and eat People, and they will fear you."

Bear went off into the woods and has since been known as a fierce animal.

Then to all walking creatures, except Coyote, and all the flying creatures, to all the Animals and Birds, all the Snakes and Frogs and Turtles and Fish, Sweat Lodge gave names, and the creatures scattered.

After they had gone, Sweat Lodge called Coyote to him and said, "You have been wise and cunning. A man to be feared you have been. This Earth shall become like the air, empty and void, yet your name shall last forever. The new Human Beings who are to come will hear your name and say, 'Yes, Coyote was great in his time.' Now, what do you wish to be?"

"I have long lived as a Coyote," he replied. I want to be noble like Eagle or Elk or Cougar."

Sweat Lodge let him show what he could do. First, Coyote tried his best to fly like Eagle, but he could only jump around, this way and that way. He could not fly, the poor fellow. Then he tried to imitate the Elk in his graceful gallop. For a short distance he succeeded, but soon he returned to his own gait. He ran a little way, stopped short, and looked around.

"You look exactly like yourself, Coyote, " laughed Sweat Lodge. "You will be a Coyote."

Poor Coyote ran off, howling, to some unknown place. Before he got out of sight, he stopped, turned his head, and stood—just like a coyote.

Sweat Lodge, left alone, spoke to himself: "All now are gone, and the new People will be coming soon. When they arrive, they should find something that will give them strength and power.

"I will place myself on the ground, for the use of the Human Beings who are to come. Whoever will visit me now and then, to him I will give power. He will become great in war and great in peace. He will have success in Fishing and in Hunting. To all who come to me for protection I will give strength and power."

Sweat Lodge spoke with earnestness. Then he lay down on his hands and knees and waited for the first People. He has lain that way ever since and has given power to all who have sought it from him.

WHY THERE ARE
NO SNAKES ON TAKHOMA

A Story from the Cowlitz People

A long, long time ago, Tyhee Sahale became angry with the People. Sahale ordered a Medicine Man to take his bow and arrow and shoot into the Cloud which hung low over Takhoma. The Medicine Man shot the arrow, and it stuck fast in the cloud. Then he shot another into the lower end of the second. He shot arrows until he had made a chain which reached from the Cloud to the earth. The Medicine Man told his klootchman and his children to climb up the arrow trail. Then he told the good Animals to climb up the arrow trail. Then the Medicine Man climbed up himself. Just as he was climbing into the Cloud, he looked back. A long line of bad Animals and Snakes were also climbing up the arrow trail. Therefore, the Medicine Man broke the chain of arrows. Thus the Snakes and bad Animals fell down on the Mountainside. Then at once it began to Rain. It Rained until all the Land was flooded. Water reached even into the Snowline of Takhoma. When all the bad Animals and Snakes were drowned, it stopped Raining. After a while the water sank again. Then the Medicine Man, and the klootchman, and the children climbed out of the Cloud and came down the Mountainside. The good Animals also climbed out of the Cloud. Thus there are now no Snakes or bad Animals on Takhoma.

DOG GOES FOR FIRE
From the Coeur d'Alene

People had a fire. Wolf had no fire. Wolf and Dog were friends. Wolf said to Dog, "Go steal a spark from the People."

Dog went to the People. They fed him and he forgot to steal the spark. That's all.

THE ORIGIN OF SUN, MOON, AND STARS
INUIT

At a time when darkness covered the Earth, a girl was nightly visited by someone whose identity she could not discover. She determined to find out who it could be. She mixed some soot with oil and painted her breast with it. The next time she discovered, to her horror, that her brother had a black circle of soot around his mouth. She upbraided him and he denied it. The father and mother were very angry and scolded the pair so severely that the son fled from their presence. The daughter seized a brand from the fire and pursued him. He ran to the Sky to avoid her, but she flew after him. The man changed into the Moon and the girl who bore the torch became the Sun. The sparks that flew from the brand became the Stars. The Sun is constantly pursuing the Moon, which keeps in the darkness to avoid being discovered. When an eclipse occurs, they are supposed to meet.

THE NORTHERN LIGHTS
INUIT

Auroras—or Northern Lights—are believed to be the torches held in the hands of Spirits seeking the souls of those who have just died, to lead them over the abyss terminating the edge of the World. A narrow pathway leads across it to the land of brightness and plenty, where disease and pain are no more, and where food of all kinds is already in abundance. To this place none but the dead and the Raven can go. When the Spirits wish to communicate with the People of the Earth, they make a whistling noise, and the Earth People answer only in a whispering tone. The Inuit say that they are able to call the Aurora and converse with it. They send messages to the dead through these spirits.

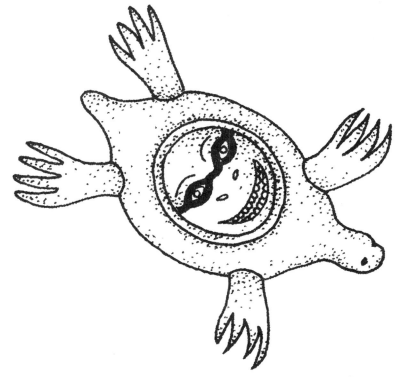

QUARREL OF THE
SUN AND MOON
A SIOUX STORY

In the days of the first grandfather, the Moon and Sun lived upon the Earth. Then they quarreled.

Said the Moon: I am out of patience with you. I gather the People, but you scatter them. You cause them to be lost."

Said the Sun: I wish for many People to grow, so I scatter them. You put them in darkness; thus you kill many with hunger." Then Sun called to the People, "Ho! Ye who are People. Many of you shall grow strong. I will look down on you from above. I will rule all your work."

Said Moon, "And I, too, will dwell above you. I will gather you when it is dark. Assembling in full numbers, you shall sleep. I myself will rule all your work. We will walk in the trail, one after the other. I will walk behind you."

COYOTE AND RATTLESNAKE
A LEGEND OF THE SIA

The Coyote's house was near the house of the Rattlesnake. The Coyote said to the Snake, "Let us walk together," and while walking he said to the Snake, "Tomorrow come to my house." In the morning the Snake went to the house of the Coyote and moved along slowly on the floor, shaking his rattle. The Coyote sat to one side, much afraid; he became frightened after watching the movements of the Snake and hearing the noise of the rattle. The Coyote had a pot of Rabbit meat cooking on the fire, which he placed In front of the Snake, inviting him to eat, saying, "Companion, eat." "No, companion, I will not eat your meat. I do not understand your food," said the Snake. "What food do you eat?" asked the Coyote. "I eat yellow Flowers of the Corn," was the reply, and the Coyote immediately began to look around for some, and when he found the pollen, the Snake said, "Put some on the top of my head that I may eat it," and the Coyote, standing as far off as possible, dropped a little on the Snake's head. The Snake said, "Come nearer and put enough on my head that I may find it." He was very much afraid, but after a while the Coyote came close to the Snake and put the pollen on his head; and after eating the pollen the Snake thanked the Coyote, saying, "I will go now and pass about," but before leaving he invited the Coyote to his house: "Companion, tomorrow you come to my house." "Very well," said the Coyote, "Tomorrow I will go to your house."

The Coyote thought much about what the Snake would do on the morrow. He made a small rattle (by placing tiny pebbles in a gourd) and attached it to the end of his tail, and, testing it, he was well satisfied and said, "This is well," he then proceeded to the house of the Snake. When he was near the house, he shook his tail and said to himself, "This is good; I guess when I go into the house the Snake will be much afraid of me." He did not walk into the house, but moved like a Snake. The Coyote could not shake the rattle as the Snake did his; he had to hold his tail in his paw. When he shook his rattle, the Snake appeared afraid and said, "Companion, I am much afraid of you." The Snake had a stew of Rats on the fire, which he placed before the Coyote and invited him to eat, saying, "Companion, eat some of my food," and the Coyote replied, "I do not understand your food; I cannot eat it, because I do not understand it." The Snake insisted upon his eating, but the Coyote continued to refuse, saying, "If you will put some of the Flower of the Corn on my head I will eat; I understand that food." The Snake quickly procured some Corn pollen, but he pretended to be afraid to go too near the Coyote, and stood off at a distance. The Coyote told him to come nearer and put it well on the top of his head; but the Snake replied, "I am afraid of you." The Coyote said, "Come nearer to me; I am not bad," and the Snake came closer and put the pollen on the Coyote's head and the Coyote tried to eat pollen; but he had not the tongue of the Snake, so could not take it from his head. He made many attempts to reach the top of his head, putting his tongue first on one side of his nose and then on the other, but he could only reach either side of his nose. His repeated failures made the Snake laugh heartily. The Snake put his hand over his mouth, so that the Coyote should not see him laugh; he really hid his head in his body. The Coyote was not aware that the Snake discovered that he could not obtain the food. As he left the Snake's house he held his tail in his paw and shook the rattle; and the Snake cried, "Oh companion! I am so afraid of you!" but in reality the Snake shook with laughter. The Coyote, returning to his house, said to himself, "I was such a fool; the Snake had much food to eat and I would not take it. Now I am very hungry," and he went out in search of food.

OWL AND RAVEN
Inuit

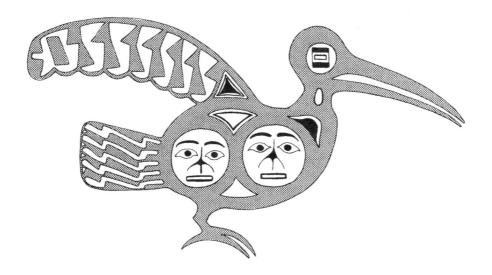

Owl and Raven were close friends. One day Raven made a new dress, dappled black and white, for Owl. Owl, in return, made for Raven a pair of Whalebone boots and then began to make for her a white dress. When Owl wanted to fit the dress, Raven hopped about and would not sit still. Owl became very angry and said, "If I fly over you with a blubber lamp, don't jump." Raven continued to hop about. At last Owl became very angry and emptied the blubber lamp over the new white dress. Raven cried, "Qaq! Qaq!" Ever since that day Raven has been black all over.

THE CREATION OF MANKIND
PIT RIVER STORY

Silver-Fox and Coyote lived together. Silver-Fox gathered some Service Berry sticks and whittled them down, working all night. The shavings were to be made into common People. The finished sticks were to be warriors and chiefs. About Sunset the next day he was ready to make them alive. They turned into People. The Silver-Fox sent them away, some in one direction and some in another. Then he and Coyote had a big feast.

But Coyote also wanted to make People, so he did everything he had seen Silver-Fox do. He gathered some Service Berry sticks and whittled them down, working all night. About Sunset the next day he was ready to make them alive. They turned into People. But right away Coyote ran after some of the women, and after a long chase caught them. But as soon as he touched them, they turned back into shavings.

HOW OLD MAN ABOVE
CREATED THE WORLD
SHASTA

Long, long ago, when the World was so new that even the Stars were dark, it was very, very flat. Chareya, Old Man Above, could not see through the dark to the new, flat Earth. Neither could he step down to it because it was so far below him. With a large stone he bored a hole in the Sky. Then through the hole he pushed down masses of Ice and Snow, until a great pyramid rose from the plain. Old Man Above climbed down through the hole he had made in the Sky, stepping from Cloud to Cloud, until he could put his foot on top of the mass of Ice and Snow.

The Sun shone through the hole in the Sky and began to melt the Ice and Snow. It made holes in the Ice and Snow. When it was soft, Chareya bored with his finger into the Earth, here and there, and planted the first Trees. Streams from the melting Snow watered the Trees and made them grow. Then he gathered the leaves which fell from the Trees and blew upon them. They became birds. He took a stick and broke it into pieces. Out of the small end he made Fishes and the Animals except the Grizzly Bear. From the big end of the stick came the Grizzly Bear, who was made master of all. Grizzly was large and strong and cunning. When the Earth was new he walked upon two feet and carried a large club. So strong was Grizzly that Old Man Above feared the creature he had made. Therefore, so that he might be safe, Chareya hollowed out the pyramid of Ice and Snow as a tipi. There he lived for thousands of snows. The Old People knew he lived

there because they could see the smoke curling from the
smoke hole of his tipi. When the foreigners came to our country, Old Man Above went away. There is no longer any smoke
from the smoke hole. The foreigners call the tipi Mount
Shasta.

CHIPMUNK AND SNAKE
NEZ PERCE STORY

Chipmunk and Snake lived together. Their fire was one long burning log. Each of them had a stick with which to poke the fire. Chipmunk poked the fire: "U ya had ya ha." Snake poked it. "Winter" was the noise he made. When the log was burned through the middle, it would be Spring. Chipmunk was hurrying it to make Spring come quicker. Snake was trying to delay it because he wanted Winter. The only time they ceased arguing was when they slept. At dawn, as soon as they woke up they took up the stick. Suddenly, the Chipmunk said, "I'll go outside and see."

She went out the door. Already the ground was clear of Snow. Small blades of Grass showed through. She nibbled them. She went in again and took up her stick to poke the fire. Snake said, "Is it clear yet?" "No, there is still Snow on the ground." Then Snake repeated, "Winter." Suddenly he said, "You smell of green grass." "No, it's that mat you smell. I just turned it over."

Outside all was green. "Tsatapi," spoke Snake. "Ya ya," said Chipmunk. Patsatsa, Chipmunk ran out. Snake said, "My! She does smell of green grass!"

Then he went out. The ground was clear. Sun was shining. Snake ate Grass and curled himself up on the ground.

The end of my road.

WOLF BOY
KIOWA LEGEND

There was a camp of Kiowa. There were a young man, his wife, and his brother. They set out by themselves to look for game. This young man would leave his younger brother and his wife in camp and go out to look for game. Every time his brother would leave, the boy would go to a high hill nearby and sit there all day until his brother returned. One time before the boy went as usual to the hill, his sister-in-law said, "Why are you so lonesome? Let us be sweethearts." The boy answered, "No, I love my brother and I would not want to do that." She said, "Your brother would not know. Only you and I would know. He would not find out." "No, I think a great deal of my brother. I would not want to do that."

One night as they all went to sleep the young woman went to where the boy used to sit on the hill. She began to dig. She dug a hole deep enough so that no one would ever hear him. She covered it by placing a hide over the hole, and she made it look natural so nobody would notice it. She went back to the camp and lay down. Next day the older brother went hunting and the younger brother went to where he used to sit. The young woman watched him and saw him drop out of sight. She went up the hill and looked into the pit and said, "I guess you will want to make love now. If you are willing to be my sweetheart I will let you out. If not, you will have to stay in there until you die." The boy said, "I will not." After the young man returned home, he asked his wife where was his little brother. She said, "I have not seen him since you left, but he went up on the hill. That night as they went to bed the young man said to his wife that he thought he heard a voice somewhere. She said,

"It is only the Wolves that you hear." The young man did not sleep all night. He said to his wife, "You must have scolded him to make him go; he may have gone back home." "I did not say anything to him. Every day when you go hunting he goes to that hill." Next day they broke camp and went back to the main camp to see if he was there. He was not there. They concluded that he had died. His father and mother cried over him.

The boy staying in the pit was crying; he was starving. He looked up and saw something. A Wolf was pulling off the old hide. The Wolf said, "Why are you down there?" The boy told him what had happened, that the woman had caused him to be in there. The Wolf said, "I will get you out. If I get you out, you will be my son." He heard the Wolf howling. When he looked up again, there was a pack of Wolves. They started to dig in the side of the pit until they reached him and he could crawl out. It was very cold. As night came on, the Wolves lay all around him and on top of him to keep him warm. Next morning the Wolves asked what he ate. He said he ate meat. So the Wolves went out and found Buffalo and killed a calf and brought it to him. The boy had nothing to butcher it with, so the Wolf tore the calf to pieces for the boy to get out what he wanted. The boy ate till he was full. The Wolf who got him out asked the others if they knew where there was a flint knife. One said that he had seen one somewhere. He told him to go and get it. After that, when the Wolves killed for him he would butcher for himself.

Some time after that, a man from the camp was out hunting, and he observed a pack of Wolves and among them a man. He rode up to see if he could recognize this man. He got near enough only to see that it was a man. He returned to camp and told the People he had seen a man with some Wolves. They considered that it might be the young man who had been lost some time before. The camp had killed off all the Buffalo. Some

young men after butchering had left to kill Wolves (as they did after killing Buffalo). They noticed a young man with the pack of Wolves. The Wolves saw the men, and they ran off. The young man ran off with them.

Next day the whole camp went out to see who the young man was. They saw the Wolves and the young man with them. They pursued the young man. They overtook him and caught him. He bit at them like a Wolf. After they caught him, they heard the Wolves howling in the distance. The young man told his father and brother to free him so he could go the hear what the Wolves were saying. They said if they loosed him, he would not come back. However, they loosed him and he went out and met the Wolves. Then he returned to camp.

"How came you to be among them?" asked the father and brother. He told how his sister-in-law had dug the hole, and he fell in, and the Wolves had gotten him out, and he had lived with them ever since.

The Wolf had said to him that someone must come in his place, that they were to wind Buffalo gut around the young woman and send her. The young woman's father and mother found out what she had done to the boy. They said to her husband that she had done wrong and for him to do as the Wolf had directed and take her to him and let him eat her up. So the husband of the young woman took her and wound the guts around her and led her to where the Wolf had directed. The whole camp went to see, and the Wolf Boy said, "Let me take her to my father Wolf." Then he took her and stopped at a distance and howled like a Wolf, and they saw Wolves coming from everywhere. He said to his Wolf father, "Here is the one you were to have in my place." The Wolves came and tore her up.

ORIGIN OF THE SACRED ARROW

A Story from the Gros Ventres

Charred Body had his origin in the Skies. There was a big village up there and this man was a great hunter. He used to go out and bring in Buffalo, Elk, Antelope until the Buffalo became scarce—they scattered out far from the village. So one day he told his close relatives, "The Buffalo seem to have gone far away from here, and I am tired of hunting them so long. Some day they may multiply again, but now I am going to build a mound to sit on and look over the country." He made a practice of going up to this mound at intervals of three or four days to survey the land and listen to its sounds. One day toward nightfall he heard Buffalo bellowing. He was excited. He could not tell from what direction the sound came. He was in the habit of changing himself into an arrow shot from a bow and thus making in one day a journey such as a man would ordinarily make in ten days. The next day he went out to the mound, changed himself into an arrow, and went in every direction, but found no buffalo. Back on the mound he again heard the Buffalo, and they seemed so close that he thought it strange he could not place them. The next day when he went out to the mound he took an arrow and stuck it into the ground, and as the ground opened up a crack, he worked the hole a little larger and, to his surprise, could look down through the hole. There below he saw Buffalo as if the Chokecherries are half ripe, and the bulls were fighting and bellowing. This was the sound he had heard.

He went back to his lodge and told his relatives that he had seen the Buffalo, thousands upon thousands, but since, if he went down below, it would be difficult to pack the meat back, he decided to go down ahead and build a dwelling and his brothers and sisters-in-law should follow afterwards. They could themselves see by looking down the hole that there would be Buffalo enough for all.

The chief of the village was named Long Arm. He was regarded as a holy man. He usually knew what was going on from day to day, Charred Body told him of the land he had found, so beautiful and plentiful in game. Charred Body said, I want to leave this place and go down there, but it will not be possible to pack the meat back up here or to drive the Buffalo up here from the Earth. So I shall go down there to live and take with me all those near relatives of mine who are bound to me like the thread of the Spiderweb, and we will make our home there." Long Arm said neither yes nor no; he uttered no word. The hunter went back to the hole, transformed himself into an arrow and flew through the air to Earth.

He came down so swiftly that as he landed on the ground the arrow point struck the Earth, and it seemed as if he were stuck there for good. The place where he landed was near Washburn by a creek some People call Turtle, but which we call Charred Body Creek. There was an evil spirit in the creek whose moccasin tops were like a flame of fire so that when he went through the forest the Cottonwood Trees would burn down. He would undo the flap of the moccasin when he went to Windward and wave it back and forth over the ground; when he tied it up again the flame ceased. This man feared the man from Heaven lest he establish villages or take away his land or even kill him, so he caused a Windstorm and set the Prairie on fire and the flames charred the arrow here and there. Hence the name "Charred Body" is derived. Since the arrow could not pull himself out, he decided to make a spring: thus he loosened himself. So he decreed that the spring would flow as long as the World should last; you can see even today where the spring is.

Charred Body established thirteen lodges. First, he looked about and found a good site and established one lodge, then another, until he had thirteen built. Then he went back into the Heavens and told what had happened and how the old man with flame about the foot had tried to kill him, how he had found the spring and how good the game was. He made it sound very attractive. He said that he went by the arrow and hence could take down only as many families as there were parts to the arrow. He would take his nearest relatives only, with their children. The groove at the end of the arrow to put the string into was one lodge. The three feathers were regarded as lodges; that made four. The two sinews bound about it were two others, making six. The three points of the arrowhead were three other lodges, making nine. The three grooves circling around the arrow in a spiral made twelve. The arrow itself was the thirteenth: there were thirteen lodges all told. The spiral is considered as Lightning; hence the arrow's power. If it does not come in contact with a bone, it will penetrate the Buffalo right through.

He called his nearest relatives and embraced them, and in embracing them he gave them the power of the arrow and encouraged them to follow him. First, he went down, then to all of those who came after he assigned lodges. When they first came down, the mysterious bodies down there knew that he was also Mysterious and they tried to kill him, but when he pulled himself out of the hole made by the arrowpoint they knew that they had no power against him. Before coming down, the People had made preparations and brought seed of Corn, Beans and so forth and began to plant on the ground by the river and to build scaffolds for drying the corn, beans, and the meat. So they lived happily for a long time. You can see today the remains of their thirteen villages, but obscured by water and the ploughing farmers. I have heard that People found arrowheads in the thirteen villages.

After a number of years, First Creator happened to come to the village. He asked some boys playing outside who was the chief. They showed him the way to the large lodge in the center which was Charred Body's lodge. He asked Charred Body how he came there and Charred Body told him. He said it was well and that he wished to make friends with Charred Body; when there were two they could talk matters over and act more effectively (than one), three were even better, but two were strong. They must therefore love one another. So they became friends, ate and talked together, and First Creator stayed in the lodge several nights before he went on again.

When he came back, he reported that there was a big village East of them whose chief had a beautiful daughter. It was the custom in that village after noon for the maidens to go along a wide path to the river for water and for the men to line up along the path and do their courting. The married women would go along the path outside the row. When a young girl came opposite a man who liked her, he would clear his throat and if the girl looked at him, it was a good sign, The next day he would ask a drink, and if she gave him a drink it was a still better sign. So People took notice, and if a girl gave a man a drink it became a matter of gossip, the parents came together to find out whether the two were industrious and able to run a household, and if everything was favorable, they were married. Now the chief's daughter had a strong will and never looked at the young men, When they tried to catch her eye she paid them no attention. "Now, my friend," said First Creator, "You are handsome, not too slender, too tall or too short. Your hair is long and beautiful. No one could find a blemish upon you. You would certainly make a hit with the girl, so let us go over and try our luck. If you can get her and be son-in-law to a great chief, you will be a renowned man."

So it was agreed, and when they came to the edge of the village to a place where the moles had dug up a mound of Earth, they began to dress themselves up. Charred Body mixed the dirt with water and daubed mud across his chin from ear to ear and upon his cheeks, brought his hair together in a big pompadour in front and stuck a plume in at the place where he tied it up. This feather the wind waved to and fro. His robe he wore open with his bow and arrows inside. Today we say of a person who combs his hair to the side in a pompadour that "he wears his hair like Charred Body."

They went to a certain lodge in the village and were kindly received. When First Creator told them who Charred Body was they said, "We have heard about him and how he had a beautiful land in the Skies and liked the country down here." When he said that they had come courting, the People said, "It is well." They went down to the path by the river and stood opposite each other and Coyote, which is another name for First Creator, said he would give a signal when the chief's daughter came so that his friend would pay no attention to the others. She came dressed in tanned white Deerskin with a robe of Elkskin from which the hair had been scraped, light and pliable as a plume. Charred Body stepped in front of her and she swerved. He turned also and she swerved again. When he was almost in front of her he said, "I wish to drink out of your cup." She said, "What you have done is not according to our custom; you should not have moved from the line but just cleared your throat, and I shall give you no drink!" "Do you make those streaks across your face in imitation of the charring?" He was angry, took out his bow and arrows and, as she turned to flee, shot her twice in the back and killed her. A tumult arose and the two visitors raced back to their own village.

Coyote warned Charred Body that he had done an evil deed and that this would not be the end of it. The chief was not likely to sit still and do nothing. He had owned the land before Charred Body came there, and Charred Body must therefore build barricades and protect himself. Charred Body paid little attention to him. "I go by the arrow and it can pierce through them," he said. "Even then," said Coyote, "You are often out hunting, and while you are away they may send out scouts and kill all in the village. More than one lodge may combine against you. You may think that you can fight them single-handed, but you have done a bad deed and this will cause your mind to stray, and while it is occupied with other things, they will overcome you. So whatever you do, don't let anything distract your attention or you may be destroyed."

Day after day, Charred Body would go and sit on the top of a hill where he had a mound and look over in the direction of the lodge where he had committed the crime. He told the young men cut up sticks for arrows and sort them out into bundles and put them under his bed. When they came back, the sticks would be already made into arrows. Soon all the young men were supplied. But he was always in deep thought, first because of the crime he had committed and second lest the village come against him. One day Coyote offered to go over to the village and find out what they were planning. He said that he would take Cornballs and Pemmican spread them on the outskirts of the village, and if anyone was wounded he would give him the food and tell him it was Good Medicine for wounds. He would pretend that he had left Charred Body because of his crime. He met them on the way in such numbers as completely to surround the village. All who had children remained. When he had passed them, on the other side of the hill, he saw Meadowlark and sent him on an errand to fly to Charred Body on his mound and tell him to prepare four barricades because a great force was coming against him to avenge his crime.

Meadowlark carried the message, but as soon as Charred Body got back to the village to prepare the barricades, he forgot all about it. The enemy employed a Holy Man to make him forgetful; the Holy Man raised his hand against him and Charred Body forgot what was to happen. Three times Coyote sent Meadowlark with the message, and three times Charred Body forgot it as soon as reached the village. The fourth time Meadowlark told him to make some sign on his body to attract attention. Charred Body stuck a bunch of Grass in his hair and went back to the village. Again he forgot the message. He went into his lodge, but his head itched; told his wife to scratch his head, and she found the Grass and said "This is the cause of your itching!" He gave a groan and sent word to the People that the next day the enemy would come against them, that they must prepare a barricade, get arrows ready and be brave even to death. He went out and cut Bog Brush, put it under his bed and commanded it to turn to June Bushes. It became a June Bush, and he peeled the bark and made more arrows.

Coyote (in the enemy's camp) said, "You have been sending out scouts but their reports are not clear. I will go my self to see what is going on." He started on a run, but he fell, knocking his foot out of joint, and claimed it was too painful to put in again and that he was now too disabled to fight with them in the attack against the village. He said, "Way down on the river they are performing rites for Medicine, so I will go there and bring back Cornballs and Pemmican." He caused an announcement to be sounded at a distance (He must have been a ventrilo-quist.) which said:

"All you who have Medicine Bags and Mysteries, come and join in this ceremony to be performed."

He told them that he had an adopted son in the enemy's camp who was Mysterious in battle. He could not be shot by an arrow and they must keep away from him. "You will find him dressed with a bladder covering his head daubed with white clay. His body will have streaks lengthwise and crosswise. His quiver is a Coyote's hide. He will wound many of you, but I will bring a hide for the wounded to lie on and feed them with Cornballs and Pemmican." As soon as he was out of sight, he threw away his crutch, set his foot again, turned into a Coyote and ran around another way into the village and became a man again. He asked after Charred Body and learned that he was making arrows. But a weasel had just been in to see Charred Body, and it had scat-tered and trampled arrows. Charred Body had been angry and struck four times at the Weasel; the fourth time I ran out and Charred Body after it. "I told him whatever happened not to allow anything to distract him!" said Coyote. "But never mind, I am here. Don't turn into women!" Charred Body's sister was at this time with child, and Coyote told her to go inside a cellar-hole, and he would cover her over so that she would not be burned.

When the battle took place, there were four among the enemy's band who had supernatural power. One had no head, but only a big mouth from shoulder to shoulder into which he sucked his enemies; another was an old woman with a basket which, wherever she turned, sucked in People or Birds of the air; a third was the man with flaming moccasins; a fourth was a Beaver (called Tail-With-a-Knife) whose tail was sharp on both sides. These four helped the enemy. Tail-With-a-Knife chopped down the barricade, Flame-Around-His-Ankle encircled the village and set it on fire. Coyote was in the thick of the battle dressed as he had described. When he saw that all was lost, he disappeared in a cloud of smoke.

Meanwhile, Charred Body was still chasing Yellow Weasel. It seems that there was a transformation of the Earth so that Charred Body found himself far to the North. Yellow Weasel said, "Look back and see your own village!" He looked and saw the smoke. He wanted to get back as quickly as possible. His eyesight would be too slow, for he would have to stop at the end of each sight, so he used his thinking power, transformed himself into thought, and wished himself back at his village. There he found the place in flames.

Now after the battle, the enemy had withdrawn and were relating their exploits. It seemed to them as if Coyote had fought in the Battle, and Coyote heard their word as he came limping back with the hide, Cornballs and Pemmican. An old Bear was appointed to discover whether Coyote had been in the battle. The way he did this was to lift up his paw and put it upon a Person, then put his paw to his nose and smell it. When Coyote entered, the paw was raised to test him, but Coyote put a cornball into the paw, saying, "You greedy fellow, you want this all for yourself!" Then he had the wounded brought in and laid upon the robe, and gave them Cornball and Pemmican. He said, "However wounded you may be yourselves, you have destroyed the village and enticed Charred Body away." And he said, "These People were just like relatives to me, and I want to go back there and walk through the place where young men and maidens formerly walked, and think about their sports and laughter and mourn there for them." So they consented and he went on his way.

Close to the village he saw Charred Body walking among the dead. As was the custom in those days, Coyote walked up to him, put his arm about his neck, and wept over him. Then he told him where he had hidden the sister, and they went to the cellar to see if she were alive. When they lifted up the hide she came out, but when she saw the desolation of the village she wept and the men with her. Coyote proposed that they have a lodge, to live in together. He faced the North, raised both eyes, and he said, "I wish for a lodge facing South furnished with bedding and all things necessary and with a scaffold in front." When they opened their eyes, there it stood just as Coyote had said. There was not food, so Coyote said, "There is all kinds of food on the hoof—, let us go out and see what we can take." They followed up the creek and killed a Buffalo, cut it up, left the backbone, head and shoulders and took the best pieces. The kidney, back gut and liver they washed to be eaten raw. These raw parts are considered a tonic today to keep one from sickness. The woman at the lodge cooked for them. She began to slice the meat and roast the ribs close to the fire and they felt themselves at home once more.

After they had lived thus from day to day, bringing in game until there was plenty, Coyote went away to the enemy's camp to see what the people were doing, promising to return again. It is an old custom with both Mandans and Gros Ventres that when a sister is alone in a house, a brother must not enter out of respect to his sister. Only if someone else is with her is it right for him to enter. Hence Charred Body did not think it right to stay alone with his sister, so he went off hunting by day to bring in choice bits of food for her and told his sister on no account to let anyone into the house if anyone should come around asking for the door. "No one can come in if you do not take out the crossbar," he said, One day when he came back from hunting, he saw his sister standing outside looking as if she were laughing, and he took the meat and waited for her, but she did not come in. This is what had happened. While he was away on the hunt she had heard a voice crying, "Tuk, tuk, tuk! My daughter, where can the door be?" She forgot what her brother had told her and undid the door for the stranger. There entered a headless monster. He said, "Place me on the West side between the pillows." She said, "Grandfather, what will you have to eat?" He said, "The best is the fat of the stomach. When I eat this fat I must have a pregnant woman lie on her back and then I place the hot fat upon her and eat in this way." The woman was frightened and only half cooked it. He held it himself to the fire, and the flames wrapped his hands but he did not seem to feel it. He made her lie down on the floor and placed the hot fat upon her. The woman screamed and twins were born as the woman died. The monster took one by the leg and threw it into the center of the lodge and said, "Lodge center, make this boy your slave!" The other he threw into the spring and said, "Spring, take this child for yours!" Then he took the doorposts which were forked and set them outside and placed the woman against them and held out her lips with two sticks as if she were laughing. Then he gathered up all the food and was gone.

When Charred Body knew that his sister was dead, he made a burial scaffold for her and by means of a rude lattice he placed her body upon it and cried bitterly. In the evening he came home and was preparing an evening meal when he heard a wee voice from the center of the lodge say, "Brother, give me something to eat." Twice this happened; then he investigated. He cut a splinter and wrapped fat into it and, using this as a torch, he looked into the dark spot from which the voice came and found a baby boy. He brought the child to his knee. This was the child who had called him "brother" (among these People a mother's brother is called "brother," a father's brother is an "uncle").

When Coyote drifted back, he found to his amazement that their sister had been killed, and he mourned her loss. One day he said, "Can't we do something for our brother here? Let us take this baby up and wish that he grow to a certain height." This is the song that Charred Body sang: First he took Sweet Grass and smoked him; then he raised him up and sang, "I want my child to grow this high!" Coyote did the same. Charred Body raised him again and sang and he became like a boy of twelve. Coyote got up and raised him and sang, "I want my brother to be the height of a man," and he became like a boy of eighteen. And at the same time, since the boys were twins, the Spring-boy attained the same height also.

Since the boy was now grown, he was left to look after the lodge when the two went hunting, and every time this happened, Spring-boy came out and played with him. The name of Lodge-boy was Atu-tish, which means, "Near-the-edge-of-the-lodge," and the Spring-boy was Ma-hash from Ma-ha, meaning "spring." He was dark and his brother was light and a little taller that Spring-boy. The two men kept Buffalo tongues strung up and wondered why they disappeared so rapidly. "Are there two of you?" they asked, but the boy denied it. They had him bite the tongue, and compared the mark left by Spring-boy's teeth, and they were different. At last, Lodge-boy confessed that he had known all the time what happened when his mother was killed by the stranger and he was taken by the leg and given to the edge of the wall as a slave, and his brother had been thrown into the spring. The brother did not recall this. Spring-boy seems to have been a kind of maverick — he did not belong to anyone. He had a long tusk and lived on water creatures and was influenced by his wild life in the Spring. If anyone tried to catch him, he would tear him to pieces with his tusk. They arranged a plan to catch him. The boys used to play with gambling sticks and a round stone with a hole bored through. The men fixed up two Buffalo hides as a kind of armor with a lace down the back to hold it tight. In the game there was to be a dispute, and when the boy got down on his knees to look and see if the ring lay on the the stick, Lodge-boy was to jump on his back, tangle up his hair and thrust in a stick to which a bladder was fastened. If he ran for the spring, they could catch him by the bladder. They then prepared a sweat lodge with hot stones and water ready, and transformed themselves into arrowheads. Spring-boy came trotting up, quick and agile, and encircled the lodge to see if there was anyone about. He complained of smelling his brother, but Lodge-boy told him that was because they had been there before going out hunting. He came into the lodge and was surprised to see the bladder; Lodge-boy told him it was used to separate the marrow from the bones. He asked about the sweatbath and was told it was for the men when they came home from hunting. They began to play, and when Spring-boy knelt down to see how the ring had fallen, Lodge-boy jumped upon him, wound his legs about his body, and the two boys rolled on the ground, and Spring-boy's tusk could be heard snapping at his brother. The two men dashed in, dragged him to the sweatbath and began to switch him, crying, "What kind of a person are you? You are a human being and should behave like one." Spring-boy cried out, "I am coming to myself!" They drew him out and examined his mouth, but the tusk still showed. Three times they returned him to the bath and poured water and switched his flesh; the fourth time the tusk had disappeared and he lay exhausted. So they fastened up his hair and thrust a stick through it, to which the bladder was attached. The moment he was released he ran to the spring and jumped in, but was unable to go under because of the bladder. After the fourth time of trying to get under water, he surrendered. They gave him water to drink, inserted two fingers into his mouth, and he vomited up all the water creatures which he had eaten and was restored to the ways of men.

Now there were four occupants of the lodge. Several days passed before Spring-boy came entirely to his senses. The men he accustomed to call, "Your brothers," and one day he said, "I wish you would tell your brothers to make a bow and arrows, two painted red and two black for me and the same for you." Lodge-boy said, "You always speak indirectly to our brothers, but we are twins. We are from the Sky. There is a big village where we came from. The chief is Long-Arm and he knows everything that is going on and is called a Holy Man. When our brother Charred Body wanted to come down here to this Earth, he asked permission, and although Long-Arm said neither yes nor no, he took it upon himself to come down here, and this had led to the destruction of all our relatives. But the Holy Man knows what is going on below there. Our brother and Coyote went courting and our brother killed the chief's daughter. So there was a fight, but our other brother Coyote stowed our mother away in a cellar, and I knew all these things that were going on. One of the formidable men who took part in the fight was a monster with no head but a big mouth from shoulder to shoulder who lives around the bend of the creek. He killed our mother, and I knew all about it and thought that you did too." Spring-boy said that, through living in the spring, he had forgotten all these things. He asked for arrows the men had made for the boys. Then they went through a ceremonial and Spring-boy said that these arrows, one painted black and one red for each boy, were kept sacred and used in emergency, and they were to have other arrows for daily use.

One day as they walked near their mother's grave, Spring-boy proposed that they use the sacred Arrows to bring their mother to life. The two boys had watched the arrow rite. When the two hunters had gone out before Sunrise, they took down the arrows from the quiver, burned Sweet Grass and sang the arrow song. They did the same for the bow, resting one end of the bow on Buffalo-bull manure while they strung it. Then they went out where their mother lay. Spring-boy placed one arrow in position, sang the arrow song and let it fly. They could see it go up into the Sky like a streak of flame. As it fell the boys cried, "Mother! Mother! Look out! The arrow is going to hit you!" The figure began to move. Spring-boy sent the third arrow, and this time the mother sat up. Lodge-boy shot the fourth arrow and the mother yawned and stretched her arms. She said, "I must have slept a long time; I feel tired." The boy set up a ladder to the scaffold and the mother came down to embrace them and said, "My Spirit has remained here and was about to return to my People when you sent the arrow. You are motherless and it is a joy that you have done this for me and my Spirit has returned to my body." When they returned to the lodge, she noticed at once how the meat was cut in strings, not in the nice flat pieces that a woman is accustomed to cut. So she ate a hearty meal. In time came Charred Body and Coyote home from hunting, and as Charred Body threw down his pack he recognized his sister and they all cried for joy, and she told him how her Spirit had pitied the children and had lingered about until it had been restored to her body by means of the Sacred Arrows.

Charred Body warned the boys that although they had more supernatural power than he had, they must never lie down to take a nap without setting four arrows in the ground, one at each of the Four Directions, and lying within the arrows with the head resting to the North or to the West (for even an ordinary person should never rest his head to the South or to the East) and they must place their moccasins to point toward the West, not toward the East, because all the Spirits go to the East. Among both Mandan and Gros Ventre a dead person is always placed with head to the East.

One day the boys went out to survey the country and they came to an old man who they knew to be Flame-Around-the-Ankle. They stood side-by-side and asked him to give them a demonstration of his power. He loosened the strings of his moccasin, let the flap fall, and they saw flames leaping. They asked him to run about a Cottonwood Tree; he trotted about a tree; he trotted about it in a circle and the tree fell over in flame. Spring-boy asked to try the moccasin. "Surely you may!" He ran about a tree, then back to his brother, and then all at once he circled the old man and burned him to ashes. Then the boys ran shouting and laughing home to their mother pretending that Flame was chasing them.

Again the boys wandered out, and as they followed up the creek, Lodge-boy said, "Brother, right in that dense timber on the side of the hill lives the monster without a head who carried his mouth on his shoulders. Let us go over and have a look at him!" They approached cautiously; then turning into Chickadees, they flew over the monster's den and, perching on a tree, began to call. They filled a water bag made out of a Buffalo paunch and had heated a stone red-hot and caused it to shrink so that they could carry it in the curve of a stick. They first got a big stone, then went into their Mysteries and rubbed it until it became small. To this day, when we heat a stone red-hot for the sweatbath we call it "The Chickadees' stone." When the monster came out and opened his mouth to swallow them, they dropped the hot stone. As it went down his gullet, he thought, "It must be their claws that scratch so!" "Enlarge,

enlarge!" called the boys to the stone. He snatched the water-bag to drink and they said, "Enlarge yourself and hold more water!" The water began to boil in his stomach and the monster burst. The boys burned up his lodge, skinned him and placed the skin on Spring-boy and ran back to the lodge as if the monster were after them. Its body was black; it had two tails and claws like a wildcat's. The mother was so delighted with the victory that she danced for joy, so from that time they dance when one wins a victory, generally the women but sometimes both women and men.

There was another mysterious spot where an old woman sucked People into a basket hung upon a post. They asked her to demonstrate her power. The woman was afraid of them, knowing that they had supernatural power. A flock of Birds was passing; she waved her basket to and fro and then to the side, and brought down the Birds into the basket. Spring-boy asked her to let him try. He took the basket, waved it as the old woman had done, and drew the woman into the basket. Thus he killed her. Great was the joy of their mother when he brought her home dead in the basket.

All those Mysterious beings lived in the vicinity of Turtle Creek, which the People called Charred Body Creek, just about a couple miles East of Washburn.

Some time later the boys heard about the Beaver-with-Tail-Like-a-Knife, who could tear open the Earth with a blow. Even today you can see where his tail struck the Earth; it looks something like a shell hole. The Beaver had sharp ears, but the boys lay in wait for him and Lodge-boy shot an arrow through his head as if it were a big Pumpkin. When the Beaver was dead they cut off the tail and brought it home.

These were the beings who lived about Washburn and had allied themselves with the enemy. There might be others living at a distance, but those who lived near were all destroyed. So their mother's brothers urged them to attempt no more such exploits, and the boys agreed that their mother's safety was now assured. They wished, however, to wander further into the country, so they told their mother not to worry if they did not return and took their leave.

While all this was going on down below, the People in the Sky became uneasy lest the boys who had killed so many Mysterious beings below come up to the Sky and kill them. So they held a council and asked Long-Arm to bring Spring-boy, who was dark and reckless, up into the Sky and put him to death. Long-Arm told them he saw nothing wrong with the boys and did not wish their death. They belonged to their own People. The father and mother had had hard treatment and they had avenged themselves justly. But the People cried out all the more against Spring-boy and Long-Arm accordingly used his magic power to throw the boys into a sleep in the Moon. That is the origin of daytime napping. The boys grew sleepy and, remembering their brother's instruction, they set up the arrows and placed their moccasins Westward with the bow and arrow beside them and went to sleep. Sun cast His direct rays upon them, making them drowsy. Then Long-Arm reached down to Earth to where Spring-boy lay and picked him up and carried him up into the air.

The People arranged for Spring-boy's death. They dug a hole and the chief bade them set up a tree there with forked branches, but all feared to cut the tree lest Spring-boy come out alive and destroy the one who cut it down. They tried to persuade the women to cut it, but they said, "if you are afraid, how much more should we weak women fear!" Then the chief decreed that a hermaphrodite should cut the tree on which Spring-boy was to be hung. As soon as Long-Arm brought Spring-boy up, the people rushed upon him and beat him until he was nearly dead. They had already prepared the form of death he was to die. A rawhide was stretched across the arms of the crotch and wound around the tree while it was wet; when dry it was much tighter. The boy's arms were lanced next to the bone and his feet through the cords, and rawhide strips were run through and brought right around the tree so that he hung by wrists and feet. After he was securely tied, they raised the tree and set it forth into the hole. They had put an Antelope hide, tanned soft, about his waist so that it hung below the knee, this on account of the number of women present. Over the tree they erected a kind of bower, the cross-pieces of which were inserted into the rawhide at the top of the tree. The whole was covered with leaves.

All this time the boy said nothing, but now he spoke: "I have been delivered into your hands and I do not think evil of you, for my mother was one of you and I do not wish to destroy you. If this were done by an enemy it would not be strange, but as you are my own People, it does not seem right for you to cause me this agony. But you need not fear me." The People did not answer; they could accuse him of nothing. (Today they do not put up a man, but kill a Buffalo and cut a strip along the back leaving the tail and raise it as if the Buffalo were angry and on the other end they put the Buffalo skull without the horns and hang this up to represent the Buffalo. They set up a bower about it and gather up the Earth into a ridge on the North side and stick Bog Bush into it, beginning at each end and leaving a place vacant between. They used to leave this space so that when boy died his body could be laid down. Today they lay there the sacred Weasels or other Animals used in the ceremony. No the ridge to the West side sits the Holy Man in a robe worn hair side out.)

For three days Spring-boy hung on the tree, then he began to get weary. Now when Lodge-boy awoke from sleep and could not see his twin brother, he was alarmed and, taking the shape of a flaming arrow, he flew over the Earth even to both sides of the Ocean, calling the name of Spring-boy and, finding nothing, he returned to the place from which his brother had vanished. There he lay looking up into the Sky, when he saw a streak of light at the point where Spring-boy had been taken through. Flying through the air he entered at the same place and saw that the land was empty where all the multitudes had flocked after Spring-boy. So he changed himself into a little boy with shaggy, uncombed hair and a big belly, who was nevertheless old enough to talk, and followed the People to the field where they were massed about the bower.

At the edge of the field was a lodge in which an old woman was sitting. He asked for food and the old woman adopted him as a grandson; he waited upon her and she was glad. All this time they could hear singing going on in the bower. He said, "Grandmother, what is going on there?" So she related the whole story of Charred Body's descent to Earth and his crime and how the People feared the boys and especially Spring-boy because he was dark of color and reckless and how they had cut the tree and what Spring-boy had said about his own People destroying him. "This is the third day and night and tomorrow at noon they will place his body on the ridge in the bower," she said, and she told how they danced in the morning, at noon and in the evening and sang ten songs in rotation, and how they could not stop dancing until the ten songs were sung or extend the dance beyond them. For a drum they used a long rawhide without hair which they beat with sticks, and the dancers whistled to the rhythm of the song. The best singers beat with sticks on four small round drums of wood covered with skin on one side like a tambourine, which were to indicate the four nights of the dance. It was difficult to remember the order of the songs correctly. These four led the singing and the whole society must sing with the leader.

So the little boy asked the woman to take him to the bower. At the door she picked him up so that he could see and asked the People to make way for her and her grandchild. They were singing a song and dancing with whistles in their mouths and shouting to the man on the tree, "Be a man for one day more." As Spring-boy looked about and saw his brother, a light shone about his head and he began to move and stretch as if he had been strengthened. Lodge-boy, fearing he would be recognized, begged the old woman take him outside.

That evening they heard again the sound of songs and dancing. An Announcer came through the village warning the young men and maidens not to sleep that night, but to keep watch lest Lodge-boy come to his brother's rescue, for the Holy Man thought when he saw the light that Spring-boy's brother must have come there to strengthen him. "My grandchild, did you hear what he was saying? He says that Lodge-boy is Here!" said the grandmother. There she was, speaking to Lodge-boy in person!

Rows of People slept at the bower to watch the place. When the old woman was snoring, the boy got up, took some Buffalo fat and went over to the place. Some slept, others were talking and moving about. It seemed impossible to reach his brother. He changed himself into a great Spider and crawled up to the post where his brother was. With the fat he greased the wounds, then he cut the thongs and they came down to the ground. There he found a stone hatchet with eyes, the very one used to cut the pole, and the Holy Man knew all about it but could do nothing because the two together were too powerful for him. Long-Arm went and placed his hand over the hole by which they passed through so as to catch them. Spring-boy made a motion with the hatchet as if to cut it off at the wrist and said, "This is the second time your hand has committed a crime, and it shall be a sign to the People on Earth." So it is today that we see the hand in the Heavens. Some People call it Orion. The belt is where they cut across the wrist: the thumb and fingers also show; they are hanging down like a hand. "The Hand Star" it is called.

The boys went back to the place where they had left the arrows sticking in the ground, pulled out the arrows, and went home to their mother. She told them that the People in the Sky were like Birds; they could fly about as they pleased. Since the opening was made in the Heavens, they may come down to Earth. If a person lives well on Earth, his Spirit takes flight to the Skies and is able to come back again and be reborn, but if he does evil, he will wander about the Earth and never leave it for the Skies. A baby born with a slit in the ear at the place where earrings are hung is such a reborn child from the People in the Skies.

While the People sang and danced about Spring-boy in the bower, he had the ten songs learned and he instituted the ceremony on Earth in order to get power from the Skies. In place of a man's body he told them to use a Buffalo skin. They should hang themselves at the wrist and tie cords to their bodies and suspend the cords to the nose of the Buffalo skull and hang there just as he had been suspended. He said, "The person who performs the ceremony in memory of me may have the picture of the Sun on his chest and the half Moon on his back. The Sun causes things to grow and the Moon causes the moisture. Since I have named the Buffalo hide as my own body, the Buffalo shall range where People are. In regard to the tree, the maidens of the village must be examined, and one who is a virgin shall cut down the tree and a young man, brave and unblemished, shall help her haul the tree to the dance place. In course of time they shall marry and their seed multiply so that the People may live and not go out of existence."

The Gros Ventre (Hidatsa) People have believed in those rites. You can see where I have been lanced across the chest in those ceremonies. They took hold of the flesh, lanced it through with a sharp knife and thrust a Juneberry stick cut about four inches long and wet with saliva through the lance-thrust and tied it with buckskin so that it would not slip off, then pushed back the chest. It hurt at first but not later. As I ran around (after being suspended to the tree) my feet would leave the Earth and I was suspended in Air. Above my head I heard sounds like those made by Spirits and I believed them to be the Spirits of my helpers.

The chief celebrant at these ceremonies has usually killed an enemy. He cuts off the hand, brings it home, skins it, removes bones and fills it with sand. After it dries he empties out the hand and wears it at the back of the neck where it flaps up and down as he dances. It represents Long-Arm's hand. He wears a hand at the back and a white Antelope hide about his loins just as Spring-boy wore it. Every night he uses the ridge of Earth as a pillow. Since Spring-boy hung on the tree three days, and it took a fourth to escape back to the lodge, the ceremony lasts four days. The men lanced have to fast. The man who sleeps with his head on the ridge is naked and sage is strewn. The ceremony is called the Sundance in some tribes, but among the Hidatsa it is the "Hide-beating."

The Boys were worried for their mother's safety and the mother for that of the boys, so they sent the two older men and the mother to join the People in the Sky and take back the hatchet and give it to the owner. The boys promised their mother to stay below and help the People on Earth in Spirit as long as the World lasted and at the end of the World she would see them again. The greasing of Spring-boy's wounds by Lodge-boy was the origin of the use of grease and tallow to heal wounds.

UNKNOWN ONE, SON OF TWO MEN
Gros Ventres

The twins now went by the name of Two Men. Their former lodge was abandoned and they roamed at will all over the country and made a permanent camp on the West side of the Missouri by Knife River. There you can see the ruins of the old village. The Two Men would come back to the village for ceremonial rites, then they would be off again. When a young man of the village performed such a ceremony, if he had a young wife he would call together all the men of the clan and deliver her to them in turn. Meanwhile they sang the Holy songs and prayed for blessings upon their daughter-in-law. Thus these Two Men were given their son's wife and they took her out and sang songs and, without having any intercourse with her, she bore them a son. As he grew, Two Men visited him in spirit as often as they could until he attained manhood. They drove the Buffalo within hunting distance of the village and assured Rain to bring good Corn crops. Then one day his father was killed in an Indian war and his mother died through miscarriage. Before dying she called in a man whom she had adopted as a brother because, though not a blood relative, he belonged to the same clan, and entrusted her son to him as a brother and her mother to him as a mother. The man accepted the charge and the woman died. She was her mother's only child. From this time on the man looked after the boy and loved him dearly. His lodge was placed close to the grandmother's, and if they went on a Winter's hunt, their camps were always beside each other. The two never quarreled; hence it is a rule that when two camps are beside each other, there is to be no quarreling or backbiting between them.

From time to time they went hunting, as the custom was, or made gardens. Sometimes before the Winter hunt the women and old men would recount the deeds of the hunters and compare their ability to find a helping Spirit or to endure bravely the torture of hanging themselves over a cliff. Then, pipe in hand, they would proceed to the lodge of some warrior who had shown himself brave and give him the charge of the Winter camp for that year.

One year the leader decided to place the Winter camp near the mouth of the Yellowstone. The people harvested their Corn and stored into cellars what Corn and Squash they could not carry. In those days, nine varieties of Corn were known, differing in color or in hardness of grain, but some of these varieties have today disappeared. Almost up to today it was the custom for heralds to go through the village four days before the start and announce the departure. In those days they depended upon Dogs for transportation and the Dogs were well fed and cared for. They were harnessed with a strap of soft fur cut from the Buffalo where the fur is thickest and fastened to poles on each side. Almost over the back was a round withe bent in a circle to which were fastened rods as in basketwork, and to this luggage was fastened. This year they made camp at Beaver Creek (on the South side of the river). Below this creek is a creek called Beardancing creek where there is a big meadow like a river flat, and here they made their fourth camp.

Unknown One was now grown to be a young man and was a good hunter for his age. As they came up the river, he was successful in killing Deer, Elk and other game so that his brother was well provided. One night he came in with only a small portion of the game he had killed and said to his grandmother, "On our way up I went in advance of the camp and saw a few herds to be sure, but the bulls looked scabby. I think it is going to be poor hunting and propose that you and I go home and I will provide for you through the Winter. But let us not tell my brother anything." So the next day he delayed starting until the camp had gone over the hill and then the two packed up and returned to the village. At a certain place where a man eloping with a girl had tried to shoot a rabbit and always missed it, hence called, "The place where the man missed the Jack Rabbit," they could look over the whole village and from one hut they saw smoke rising. The boy said, "Grandmother, there must be someone remaining in the village." "That must be the man who broke up the gambling-stick. I have heard that although he is only a middle-aged man he has been poisoned and cannot use his legs." It was in fact this man; he had remained with his wife and daughter, a girl of marriageable age. She ran out joyfully to meet them and the young man shared his game—the ham of the Deer, a rib, and such pieces also as are eaten raw. They insisted that the two must share their lodge, the cornmeal was already cooked, and bullhide was placed for the old lady to sit upon.

Early next morning at dawn Unknown One rose and went hunting. About daybreak he came to a river where the antelope crossed, killed four and carried back the parts eaten raw and as many ribs as he could carry. In those days they had a big log of wood burning all night covered with ashes and the ashes were brushed away to kindle a fire in the morning. The old man was overjoyed. "I had thought that we would make snares and catch Snowbirds, but now we are to be provided for the whole Winter," he said. Toward Spring the old man proposed to his wife that as they liked the young man, he should become their son-in-law. The wife consented. They proposed the match to the old woman, promising to look after her until the day of her death. She told her grandson of the proposal, but he refused to consent. "I should be the laughing-

stock of the People if I should marry before performing any warrior's deed!" The old woman begged him to consider her loneliness, but he refused to yield. Three times the proposal was made, three times he rejected it. The fourth time was the last chance. The old lady sat by the fire mending. She told him how old she was and how she could not live much longer, how his own

mother would wish the match, and even threatened suicide unless he would marry the girl; so rather than this happen he promised to marry. The old people rejoiced at the news. All was prepared and there was a marriage. The young girl loved the man dearly, as he was a handsome fellow, and she herself was a beauty. Her father gave to his daughter for his son-in-law his Eagle-tail ornament made out of twelve feathers, and the young man was well pleased with it and hung it up in its case.

One day as he was out hunting, he shot a Deer and was skinning it when he saw two men whom he recognized as his fathers. The men told him that in order to honor their daughter-in-law, they were driving down a herd of Buffalo from the North and among them a White Buffalo out of which to prepare a robe for their daughter-in-law to hang on the scalp-pole in front of the lodge. They bade him cover the fire so that there should be no flame, muzzle the dogs so that they would not bark. Also he must burn incense. The wife prepared a dish of Corn cooked with fat and prepared the father-in-law's tobacco for smoking (by greasing leaves and drying them on the fire). At night as the Stars appeared one by one in the Heavens they would come to visit the lodge. So all was done as directed and at the appointed time Two Men lifted the bullhide at the door and entered the lodge. The coals burned without flame and the lodge was dim. Unknown One took the pipe from a square of buffalo hide and passed it to Spring-boy who lit it at the coals and smoked by inhaling the Sweet Smoke; it was then cleaned out, refilled and passed to Lodge-boy. Unknown One then divided the Eagle-feathers, giving six to each, which they stuck in their hair. It is for this reason that feathers are valued today by the People. Unknown One dished out the sweet Corn and in no time they had cleaned out the pot, neglecting the meat which was there in abundance. After smoking again, the visitors advised them to bring in ice and drinking water in preparation for a heavy fog which would last four days while the buffalo were being brought in; then they left the lodge.

Two Men had observed that the father-in-law was lame, and Spring-boy now agreed to doctor the man. They came to the Lodge a second time. Spring-boy had the fire rekindled with split wood and water brought in. He dipped up some of the water into his mouth and gargled four times. Then he took more water into his mouth, chewed up some black medicine and going over to the man, took hold of the leg by the ankle, lifted it up and blew the finely chewed medicine four times from the man's leg up to his hips. Something was seen twitching in the man's leg. Spring-boy reached into the instep and drew out a male bull Snake and placed it in the ashes. Lodge-boy did the same and drew out a female bull Snake from the left leg, which he laid on the ashes beside the other. He told the husband and wife to tie cords to the Snakes, spit black medicine over their legs and draw the Snakes out on the snow and leave them with their heads pointing to the West, then cleanse their hands with Sagebrush and lay Sagebrush at the rear, pointing to the West. The man was now perfectly well. All that night they kept a light in the house lest the Snakes escape, and the next morning they took them far outside the village and left them on the snow as directed. Four times the young man would have stopped to leave them, and four times the wife insisted that they should be carried farther from the village.

When the two returned they hauled the ice as directed and placed it on blocks of wood close to the door. Four days the fog lasted when they must muzzle the Dogs and keep inside. Voices were to be heard like those of Women, which were Spirit voices. After four days they could see through the smoke hole that the Sky was clear. Outside they found all the scaffolds throughout the village loaded with meat, the scaffold outside their own door as well, and on the scalp-pole hung the white Buffalo hide. This the mother took down immediately to tan. Buffalo were to be seen roaming about everywhere. The old man was delighted. Day by day he went through the village to drive the Ravens and Magpies from the meat. Their own store of meat the family put away, the old grandmother helping as she could. The bones were then crushed with a stone hammer over a flat stone, the grease melted out and stored in Buffalo bladders. When Spring came, the man erected shelters over the scaffolds to protect the dried meat. One day the Two Men came to the boy and told him that the People were returning and would camp that night by the Little Missouri. They would send four runners to the village and these must be well fed and given bundles of meat to carry back, for the People were famishing. So they got a good rib

roasting slowly by the fire to feed the runners and give them bundles of jerked meat to carry back to the others. Just about where the ferry is today, that is where the camp began, and it was stretched West to the upper crossing. The next day there was a string of young men and women all the way into the village, some hurrying to preserve the meat and others to take food back to the others. Old People hobbled along on their canes eager to see what had happened. Soon the whole village was lively with People.

Unknown One was hunting and his two fathers came to him. They told him that they could not come to his lodge now, for his father-in-law was the kind of man in whose lodge men congregate. They warned him that although he had Mysterious power, he was nevertheless human and the evil spirits would not fear him as they did his two fathers. Whatever happened therefore, he must never allow himself to feel fear or they would get the better of him.

He was more cautious after this and formed the habit of going up on the lodge and looking off in a Southwesterly direction over the village. One day he saw a big Buffalo on a ridge headed toward the river and, thinking to get a shot at it as it came to the river, he took his bow and arrows, explained to his wife where he was going and hid himself in a ravine in the Buffalo's path. As it came along he was surprised to see that at times its body appeared to contract. He shot, but the animal contracted its body so that all the ribs showed, and the arrow fell off harmlessly. The Buffalo ran; he pursued. Four times he shot, but the arrow had no effect. He followed it up a coulee, came to a lodge, and was amazed to see the Buffalo change into a human being and walk into the lodge. "I told you to bring him along; did you bring him?" said a voice inside. "Yes, he's standing outside," said another voice. "I had all the points arranged where he was to shoot, but the four shots were the limit of my power. With every shot I drew the distance toward me and succeeded in getting him here." "Son, enter in!" said the first voice.

Inside was a great serpent with a concave Snake face, a big mouth, four legs with claws and a tail coiled in a heap. As the boy entered there came a hissing sound and flames shot forth. This so frightened him that he went around the fireplace, and because of this fear he lost his memory and could not recall his own Mysterious power. A man reproved the Snake and said, "Only if he brings home no game or tries to escape are you to kill and eat him!" and to the youth he explained how the Buffalo had drawn in the country at every shot with its paw so that he was now in the North country in a land of springs and running water where it was useless for him to try to escape. His task was to hunt Deer and bring home the whole body without skinning it. He must then skin it and boil the guts and head for the serpent and feed him without tasting a bit himself. Then he must fill the pouch with water and raise it to the Snake's lips, throw out the remainder and taste no drop himself. This man had been in the fight with Charred Body and formed an alliance with the chief whose daughter he had killed. He knew that Unknown One was his enemy's grandchild and had sent the Buffalo to draw him to his lodge.

The boy went out, shot and killed a Deer, cut down the skin over the shinbone and took out the bone, leaving the hoof,

which he brought crosswise through a slit cut in the skin so that he could hang the deer over his shoulder. The Snake hissed loudly as he came in, and even when the man quieted it, still it humped its back and grumbled. The boy saw no way of escape. He skinned the Deer in the customary manner by cutting the throat and drawing out the insides. These he threw to the Snake and watched him swallow them down without chewing just like feeding grain to a threshing machine. He roasted ribs, brought pieces of board and placed them in front of the man and laid cooked meat before him. When the man had eaten, he threw every bone into the fire so that the boy should not get a taste. After this the boy took the water-bag made of Buffalo pouch laced into a kind of kettle, carried it to the river and, wading out to the middle where the water ran clear and cool, he brought it back filled to the brim and lifting it with great difficulty to the man's mouth, gave him what he could drink and poured out the rest outside without tasting a drop. Then he took string and a stone axe and went after firewood. He was commanded to bring no rotten sticks but dry wood fit for firewood and to drink no water on the way. "Should you disobey me in the slightest in one of these commands," said the man, "you will die. This Earth with us is like a small dish out of which you cannot escape." So during his captivity the boy had little liberty except when out hunting; it was just as if he were shut up in a penitentiary. During the night the fear of the serpent kept him awake. The man slept on the left of the door, the boy on the right, the bull near the center. Under him there was not even straw and he had neither pillow nor robe.

For three days the same thing happened. On the fourth day he had become so weak that when he got the Deer on his back he was unable to lift it. As he lay on his back crying he saw a bright light pass across the Sky and heard a voice crying, "Where are you?" The Two Men had become alarmed and were out looking for him. With their backs against each other they were traveling all over the Sky. They had searched the mountains in the West, the Ocean, but had not thought of the North. The boy suddenly realized that he also had Mysterious powers but had allowed his Mind to become distracted. He got up, took up his arrow that slid the farthest and wet it across his mouth to indicate that it was the voice that the arrow was to carry, with a call for help. Had he not wet it, the arrow would have gone through the air with a flash of light but carried no sound with it. He strung his bow, tested the string, strung the arrow and called out twice to Spring-boy and Lodge-boy, "Hehh-h! Heh-h-h!" Then he let go the arrow and it shot through the air like a flame with a sound tearing and came down again beside the boy. The Two

Men followed it and he was overjoyed. Lodge-boy looked at him sadly, thinking how he must have suffered, but Spring-boy laughed and asked how he could possibly have become so emaciated. "Whoever it is, the enemy shall not escape my hand today," he promised.

The boy related his story and as he laid his ear against the Deer he heard a ringing sound in his right ear. This is the sign of glad news; a ringing sound in the left ear is a sign of bad luck. The men told him that the serpent had caused him to lose his wits and this ringing sound was the return of his consciousness of power. The men shot a fat old Buffalo for the boy to eat. They cut out the leg bone and used it to strike the backbone loose so that they could cut up the ribs. They told the boy to drink four times of the blood from the ribs and gave him a piece of the raw liver to eat. Then they accompanied him to the lodge and told him to go in as usual, but when the man had finished drinking to throw the rest of the water upon him and they would enter and take care of the situation.

All was done as they had said. They bound the serpent from its head to its tail and threw it into the fire. They shot the man and burned him with the serpent. But the Buffalo they spared. This was the leader of the Buffalo who had brought in the herd for the boy's marriage feast, but he had been taken into captivity by the man. He promised to do them no harm, only when they made sacrifices and did not perform the ritual correctly would he allow them or their ponies to be gored. Then the two set the boy between them, Spring-boy to the right and Lodge-boy to the left, and made a leap and landed beside the river near the village. All the family who had been mourning for him rejoiced. The young man became a great chief.

THE BIRD THAT TURNED THE MEAT BITTER

A Mandan Story

Looking about the lodges in the village, Coyote saw strings of jerked meat, but the People were lean. He asked why this was. The People said, "When we go hunting, only the fastest butchers can get their meat home in good condition. There is a Raven which flies over calling 'Get bitter! Get Bitter' ('gi-ba' in Mandan) and the meat turns bitter." Coyote asked for a sample. He chewed but he could not swallow the meat, it was so bitter. He said, "I must have this thing righted." He sent the young girl after firewood and had it piled ready to light, first laying down manure because it keeps the flame a long time. Then he had the men get timber rope and make a snare. He filled up his pipe and asked help of his fellow creatures. The big Spider came to his aid, and he lighted the pipe for the Spider to smoke. Now the Raven lived in a hollow tree out of which it flew when the men were butchering. Big Spider said, "It is easy to snare that Bird. Be ready to snare him into the fire and let him burn. Some of his feathers will fly into the air and turn into Birds. When you see a White Raven fly out and cry, 'At the end of the World there shall be seen a White Raven as a sign that the World is coming to an end,' that will be the last of it."

They sent out young men into the hills scouting. These reported Buffalo. They made ready for the hunt. The fastest runners went ahead to encircle the herd. Buffalo always run toward the Wind, but the runners drove them toward the other hunters. These formed a corral where they slaughtered the whole herd. The men with large families packed meat home; others followed behind.

Meanwhile, some watched by the hollow tree. When the Bird came out, before it could cry, Coyote caught it by the neck and pulled it to the ground. It had the head of a man and the body of a Bird. The face was human but it had no hair. The body had wings and a long neck. It was a frightful thing to see. Coyote clubbed the Bird and threw it into the flames. Feathers flew up and turned into Birds and flew away. The unburned bones Coyote crushed with his club. Finally out flew a White Raven and said, "When the World is about to end I will come to you again!" So Coyote told the People that was to be a sign to them.

SENDEH CHEATS THE SOLDIER

A Kiowa Story

Sendeh was going along. He met someone who he had never seen before. They both stopped, and Sendeh greeted him. He said, "I do not know you, but I think I have heard about you. You are the man who cheats everybody." Sendeh answered, "Yes, I am he who cheats, but I have left my Medicine at home, about four hills away. So I cannot cheat you." The man said, "That makes no difference. If you are the one who cheats, you can cheat me without your Medicine." "I cannot cheat you without my Medicine. I wish I had it, I would cheat you." Sendeh said to the soldier, "If you want me to cheat you, loan me your Horse and I will go and get my Medicine and come back and cheat you." So the soldier said, "All right, I will loan you my Horse, but you must come right back with your Medicine." So Sendeh got on the Horse. As he rode off he secretly punched him so he balked. Sendeh said, "This Horse won't go. Maybe he is afraid of me. Loan me your hat." The soldier gave him the hat. Sendeh punched him again, the Horse balked. "This Horse is afraid of me. Lend me your coat." Sendeh got on the Horse. He punched him secretly again and turned back and told the soldier he might as well let him have his blanket. "I think it would be well to give me your quirt. "All right, here is the quirt, too. Make haste, get your Medicine and come back and show me you can cheat me." The Horse went forward. Sendeh looked back and said, "Soldier, I have already cheated you. I have all your things. I have no Medicine. Now you go your way, and I will go mine."

JAY'S SKINNY LEGS

A Flathead Story

The chief had a daughter who was old enough to marry. He informed the young men that one with the strongest legs could have her. Coyote showed how long and fast he could run and claimed the girl. Bear flexed his leg muscles to show how big and strong they were, and he claimed the girl. Jay sneaked off into the woods where he gathered some black Moss that hangs from trees. He wrapped the Moss around his legs to make them look large. The chief was fooled by his trick and proclaimed him the winner. Jay had to carry his new wife across a stream in order to reach his tepee, and the water softened the moss so it fell from his legs. When he climbed the bank on the opposite side of the stream, everyone saw his little skinny legs, and they all laughed.

THE FINDING OF THE TSOMASS
A Legend of Vancouver Island

Near thirty miles from where Alberni pours her crystal stream out of the the mighty fjord that cleaves Vancouver's Island nigh in twain, a tribe of Natives lived. Their village nestled at the foot of wooded hills, which everywhere on this indented coastline rise straight up from out the North Pacific. They were a powerful tribe, E-coulth-aht by name, seven hundred strong, with many fighting men, and many children who played upon that shore. I think even now I hear the echo of their voices around the bay, and how marvelously clear an echo may be, among the inlets of that rockbound coast! I have heard my call flung back from side to side alternately, till it was lost among the rocky heights and ceased to be.

Across the bay from where the Natives lived ran a stream, called Po-po-moh-ah. Here every Autumn, when the Salmon came, they stayed and caught the Fish for Winter use. Yet

strange to say these ancient E-coulth-ahts seemed unaware that at their very doors, a Nature-hewn canal had its entrance. One fine September morning Ha-houlth-thuk-amik and Han-ah-kut-tish, the Sons of Wick-in-in-ish or, as some say, Ka-kay-un, accompanied by their father's slave, See-na-ulth, were paddling slowly to Po-po-moh-ah, when half across the bay near Tsa-atoos they saw dead Salmon floating on the tide.

The Salmon had spawned, and is it not strange to think that this, the king of Fish, should struggle up the rapid tumbling streams for many miles, against strong currents, over falls where the water breaks the least, perchance to fall within the wicker purse of People's traps placed there so cunningly to catch them if they should fall back? And even if they escape the traps and find the gravel bar where they four years before began their life, and having spent themselves in giving life, sicken and die, their bodies even in death give sustenance to Gulls and Eagles circling around those haunts.

"These Fish have come from where fresh water flows, so let us follow up from whence they came. Let Quawteaht direct our course, and we shall find new streams where Salmon are in plenty and win great glory in our tribe." Thus spoke the sons of Wink-in-in-ish, and they turned the bow of their canoe upstream and followed where the trail of Salmon led, to the broad entrance of that splendid fjord.

Soon they paddled by the harbor U-chuck-le-sit, long famed for its safe anchorage and quiet retreat, when Winter storms lash the waters of the sound. Leaving this quiet harbor on the left, they followed where the wider channel led to Klu-quilth-soh, that dark and stormy gap, where People say the dreaded Chehahs dwell among the rocky heights — "The Gates to Hell," and when men seek to pass those gates, the Chehahs blow upon them Winds of evil fates from North and

South and East and West. The water boils in that great witch-es' pot, People seek a sheltered beach in vain — no beach is there; no shelter from the storm. The mighty cliffs frown down relentlessly; the Whale She-she-took-amuck opens his great jaws and swallows voyagers, at which the Chehahs laugh, and their wild laughter, Klu-quilth-soh's heights re-echo far away.

In this eventful day, the evil Chehahs were absent from their home and the Yukstees Wind blew not too strong to cause the waves to dash along in wild commotion, and after paddling uneventfully through Klu-quilth-soh, the three E-coulth-ahts stopped beside Toosh-ko. Looking back they could see Nob Point, which hid their home from view—it was as if the mountains which formed those stormy gates had closed and barred them in.

"What Chehah," they cried, "has lured us within this inland sea and shut those gates? A-ha-A-ha!" they called with anxious cry, and prayed Kah-oots to save them from all dangers. To the Saghalie Tyee, the chief above, they also prayed to potlatch kloshe to guide them, and guard them from the evil Chehahs hovering around. After the relief of prayer, their Spirits rose, and once again the splashing of their paddles marked their onward progress.

Soon they glided by Hy-wach-es Creek and, rounding Wakah-nit, they came in view of the great valley where Tso-mass flows. At once they ceased from paddling to gaze with

pleasure on that favored land, and as they looked they heard the sound of song from up the river valley. The evening fell, the pleasant Yukstees Wind blew more faintly, and as it passed away, over those calm inland waters swelled again the sound of many voices chanting songs.

"There are People dwelling there," they said. "It would be well if we delayed until morning." Agreeing to this plan, they crossed the channel and camped at Klu-quilth-coose.

Next morning while the grass was damp with dew, and long before the U-ah-tee Winds had ceased, the sons of Wick-in-in-ish, hearing again the quaint alluring song, took their canoe and paddled on, to where between two grassy slopes, the Tsomass ends. When they approached the river mouth, they saw extending from the bank a Salmon trap, and even today the People will show at Lupse-kup-se some old rotten sticks, which they affirm formed part of that same trap. The land was green, the wild Duck's quack was heard among the reeds which edged the river bank while flocks of Geese were feeding on the grass which grows thickly upon the tidal flats, the flats the People call Kwi-chuc-a-nit.

Upon the Eastern bank the young men saw a wondrous house, which far surpassed their father's lodge at home beyond the hills in Rainy Bay, in size of beams and boards. The sons of Wick-in-inish were afraid and would have turned the bow of their canoe homebound, but from the house they heard a woman call. "Oh come and stay with us, go not away. Our land is full of all the riches Nature gives; our woods are bright with o-il-lie most luscious to the taste; on yonder hill the nimble au-tooch feed; in every stream the silver Salmon swim, so come within our lodge with us and stay awhile." Hahoult-thuk-amik was mesmerized by the sweet welcoming and entered in, where the Klootsmah said to him, "We welcome thee strange one unto our lodge, for we have never seen a man before."

Now Han-ah-kut-ish was alarmed and much afraid that if his brother listened to the Klootsmah and was attentive to her blandishments, he would forget the mission in which they were engaged; therefore he called to him to come, and after much persuasion the elder brother left the lodge and joined the younger and the slave See-na-ulth, and together they paddled up the stream to Ok-sock-tis opposite the present village of O-pit-ches-aht. Across the river there were houses in which more Klootsmah lived, but at this time they were employed in gathering Kwa-nis in the land behind, and when the young men sought them out, they were afraid, and all but one took flight, escaping to the woods. This one had no fear, but coming near to Ha-houlth-thuk-amik, besought him with favor to look on her, but Han-ah-kut-ish again reminded him that they had not as yet attained the object of their quest.

Still further up the stream they went, until they came to where they found the Ty-see Salmon spawning on the gravel bars. Believing they had found the object of their search, they camped the night at Sah-ah-hie. All through the darkness they listened to the rushing of the Fish, when the gaunt and savage males with flattened heads and upper jaws curved like a hook about the lower, and armed with dog-like teeth, fought for the females of their choice. With great satisfaction they heard the wallowing of the Fish, as with their heads and tails they formed the elongated cavities in the gravel in which to lay their eggs. Then Ha-houlth-thuk-amik declared that this, the Tsomass River, was the source from which the dead Fish came which they had seen when paddling to Po-pomoh-ah.

To Lup-see-kup-se they returned next day, and there they saw, among the women in the lodge, the girl who spoke to them when they had landed on the river opposite Ok-sock-tis. Then Hahoulth-thuk-amik, desiring to convey her home with him, took her aside and said, "If thou wilt come with me, say not a word, but unbeknown make haste and leave the house, and run across the point which forms the Eastern bank where this the

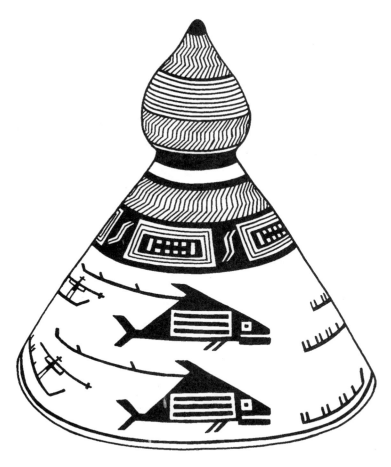

Tsomass River joins the inland sea, then hide thyself until we take thee in, as we are paddling home."

The Klootsmah did as she was told, and as the young men passed she jumped within the canoe and was away with them. That night they stayed at Chis-toh-nit not far from Coleman Creek, so named because in later days a man of that name took up some land and dwelt there some little while.

Next morning the Klootsmah said to Ha-houlth-thuk-amik, I am Kla-kla-as-suks and I am now thy rightful wife, and therefore I desire to make of thee a famous hunter of Whale, so come with me and climb the mountain called Kuk-a-ma-com-ulth where high above the timber line the green grass grows, and I will get for thee an Ow-yie Medicine."

They climbed the mountains and she secured for him the Medicine so desired by all who hunt the Whale, and early next morning blown by a strong U-ah-tee Wind, they started from Pomo-moh-soh, and when they came to Klu-kwilth-soh, they found the gates wide open and passed safely through between the frowning cliffs, arriving home before the break of day.

Then Ha-houlth-thuk-amik aroused his father who was still asleep and bade him light a fire, and when the fire was lit he told him how they ventured up the unknown way, between high cliffs, where they had lost all sight and sound of Rainy Bay. He told of the Tsomass Land, and the Salmon stream which far eclipsed their own Po-po-moh-ah, and then described the great and wondrous house, where the Klootsmah dwelt, and how they sang to him, "Yah-hinin-ay." He told him also of Kla-kla-as-suks, the Klootsmah who had left her home to be his rightful wife.

Then Wick-in-in-ish sent for all the tribe, and when they were assembled in his lodge, he told to them the story of the Tsomass land. Among the braves was much talking, and after speeches from the lesser chiefs, it was decided that the next day before Sun had cast His shadow North and South, with Yuk-stees Wind, they would set sail for Tsomass land.

That day in every house, in varied occupation, each family busied. The Cedar boards which form the sides and roof of all their houses were piled upon canoes. Atop of these were set their household goods, the mats of Cedar bark, the wooden tubs in which they boiled their Fish, the spears of flint, their hooks of bone, their fishing lines of Kelp, and mattresses of Water Reed. Large quantities of Clams and Mussels, also salmon cured by smoke they took with them, for Wick-in-in-ish

planned to give a great potlatch to the strange tribe of girls, from which his eldest son had chosen one to be his wife.

Next morning long before Sun had reached the Zenith they had set sail for Tsomass land. It truly must have been a sight to see, that fleet of dark canoes piled high with all the wealth of that great tribe, as with the sails of Cedar bark filled with the Yuk-stees Wind, they glided by the green and rocky shores which led them inland to the pleasant Tsomass land. Before the shadows of the night had spread among the gloomy conifers, the dark canoes had rounded Wak-a-nit when, taking down their sails of Cedar bark, they paddled silently close to the shore.

When near Tin-nim-ah, where the People say they find good stone for sharpening arrow points, they rested on their paddles and first heard the women singing in their Cedar lodge. Then Wick-in In-ish addressed his tribe. "My children we have sailed for many miles, and our little ones are hungry and weary. Let us sojourn near this old Spruce."

Thus they encamped near the conifer and called the place Toha-a-muk-is after the Spruce they were afraid to touch. Water they carried from near Kak-mak-kook, named from the Alders growing round the streams. All through the night they heard the Salmon splash to free themselves, so many People say, from Sea Lice clinging to their silver sides, and their hearts were happy with that refrain, which spoke to them of great supplies of food.

Early next day, before the forest trees were gilded by the glorious rising Sun, the People heard the call of many Birds and looking Northward where the Tsomass flows forth from the mist, which in the early morning hangs like a veil of gauze among the trees, they saw a flock of Sandhill Cranes appear. They flew far above their heads and, gradually ascending to the Sky, vanished from their sight. These were the maidens, so the People say, who left behind them all this lovely land for regions unexplored, taking with them both Clams and Mussels. This is the reason People give for the lack of these Shell-Fish now, upon the shores of the great inland sea. The maidens also took the Kwa-nis bulbs, but as they flew they dropped a few upon the ground; hence the Kwa-nis bulb is still found in Tsomass land.

Wick-in-in-ish, with his sons, now made haste to paddle to the river mouth but lo, the house was gone, no sign of it was left, and with it all the Klootsmah tribe had fled. Then he turned to Hahoulth-thuk-amick and said, "This is thy land, and this thy future home shall be: thou and thy chosen one Kla-kla-as-suks shall dwell therein, and may thy children be many."

Illustration Credits

These important books from Adolf Hungrywolf are
available from your local bookstore.

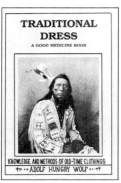

Traditional Dress
$12.95 US
978-1-57067-147-0

Blackfoot Craftworker's
Book
Adolf & Beverly
Hungrywolf
$11.95 US
978-0-913990-80-3

Pow-Wow Dancer's &
Craftworker's
Handbook
$19.95 US
978-1-57067-190-6

TheTipi
$17.95 US
978-1-57067-174-6

Mountain Home
$14.95 US
978-0-920698-54-9

Teachings of Nature
$8.95 US
978-0-913990-75-9

Also available from:
Book Publishing Company
PO Box 99
Summertown, TN 38483

1-800-695-2241
Please include $3.95 per book additional for shipping.